D0386375

With All Disrespect

Books by Calvin Trillin

KILLINGS

THIRD HELPINGS

UNCIVIL LIBERTIES

FLOATER

ALICE, LET'S EAT

RUNESTRUCK

AMERICAN FRIED

U.S. JOURNAL

BARNETT FRUMMER IS AN
UNBLOOMED FLOWER

AN EDUCATION IN GEORGIA

WITH ALL DISRESPECT

More Uncivil Liberties

by

CALVIN TRILLIN

Ticknor & Fields

NEW YORK

1985

Library of Congress Cataloging in Publication Data

Trillin, Calvin.
With all disrespect.

1. United States — Politics and government — 1981–
Anecdotes, facetiae, satire, etc.   I. Title.
E872.T75   1985   973.92′0207   84–26731
ISBN 0–89919–353–6

Printed in the United States of America

s 10 9 8 7 6 5 4 3 2 1

The pieces in this book first appeared as columns in *The Nation*,
except "Invitations," which appeared in *Vanity Fair*.

In memory of Marshall Dodge, American humorist

Contents

Introduction / 1
Damaged Goods / 6
Small Leaks / 11
Navasky as Male Model / 15
Voodoo Economics: An Eyewitness Account / 20
Moral Suasion for Grownups / 25
The Gout: A Reassessment / 30
Pinko Problems / 35
The Mailbag / 40
Neediest Case / 45
Oratory of the Islands / 50
Ouch! / 55
The Novelist Revealed / 60
The Nixon Library / 65
The 401st / 70
Harold the Committed / 75
Confessions of a Dupe / 80
My Tuxedo / 85
Too Soon to Tell / 90

Contents

Success Stories / 95

Invitations / 100

Investment Opportunities / 106

Urban Mass Transit / 111

Seder Splitsville / 116

Getting Serious / 121

Not Loony / 126

Mo. / 131

Bonjour, Madame / 136

Pinkos at Rest / 141

Marc Rich and I at Camp Osceola / 146

Marc Rich and I at Camp Osceola — Really / 151

Navasky as Felon / 156

Bicycle Mishap / 161

The Buck Stops Over There / 166

Alice as Tamperer / 171

Disengagement / 176

Beautiful Spot / 181

Nuclear War: My Position / 186

Rejected Briefer / 191

Low Visibility / 196

I Say! / 201

Loony / 206

Baker Redux / 211

Foreign Relations / 216

Line of the Day / 221

Bananas, Presliced / 226

With All Disrespect

Introduction

I HAVE BEEN ASKED a number of questions about being a columnist for *The Nation*, almost all of them embarrassing. Most often, I am asked if I'm still being paid "in the high two figures" for each column. This question is the result of a misunderstanding. In the introduction to *Uncivil Liberties*, I reported that the editor of *The Nation*, the wily and parsimonious Victor S. Navasky, had asked me to write a regular column and that I had agreed, even after he said he was thinking of paying "something in the high two figures" for each piece. I agreed to do the column all right, but I considered the phrase "high two figures" open to interpretation, particularly after I realized that Navasky thought it could be defined as sixty-five dollars. I told Navasky that on money matters he would have to speak to my high-powered agent, Robert (Slowly) Lescher. Then I called Slowly to express some thoughts on how the negotiations should be conducted. "Play hardball," I said. Slowly got him up to a hundred dollars.

Ever since the book was published, of course, the wily and parsimonious Victor S. Navasky has complained to me that it portrays him as the sort of person who pays columnists only sixty-five dollars a shot when in fact he is going a full one hundred— or what I prefer to think of as a century. Ironically, it was Navasky who insisted that I promise never to reveal that he finally agreed to come across with a C-note for each column. "It might give the other fellows ideas," he said. I promised.

While I was on the book tour for *Uncivil Liberties*, a newspaper reporter — this is someone who is actually paid to come up with embarrassing questions — asked me how I would describe *The Nation*. I thought for a long time about that one. "Pinko," I finally said. "I would describe *The Nation* as pinko."

"Surely you have more to say about it than that," he said.

I thought for a long time again. "Well," I said, "I would describe it as a pinko magazine printed on very cheap paper. It's this sort of magazine: if you make a photocopy of your piece, the copy is a lot better than the original."

The reporter left it at that, but I can imagine the questions that might have followed if he had been one of those pushy post-Watergate snoops who insist on getting at the truth. "In that case," he would have said, "why do you write a column for *The Nation*?"

Oddly enough, that happens to be a very easy question for me to answer: I write for *The Nation* because it's the closest magazine to my house. I live in Greenwich Village, and when I first started doing the column *The Nation* had its offices only a few blocks away, in an appropriately seedy building on Sixth Avenue. I used to walk the column over, picking up my laundry at Mr. Yee's on the way. I liked that. It was homey. It had the reassuring feel of what the defense analysts in Washington might call a nice uncomplicated delivery system. Then *The Nation* moved six or eight blocks uptown to slightly flashier offices, on Thirteenth and Fifth. It was still an easy bike ride from my house. In a pinch I could walk it, although I didn't really like carrying my laundry all that way. When Navasky asked me what I thought of the new offices, I said, "You're pushing it. We don't deliver out of the Village."

Listening to that, the hardnosed reporter would get the look such reporters get when they figure the quarry is just about treed. "Are you trying to tell me," he'd say, "that if a magazine devoted to furthering the cause of supply-side economics opened a block from your house, you'd do the column for them?"

"I'd just as soon not say," I would reply forthrightly. I think it's best to be honest about these things.

Sure, I would always be held in a certain amount of suspicion by people who ran a supply-side magazine — *Safety Net,* I suppose it might be called, or maybe *The Trickle-Down News.* On the other hand, I'm held in a certain amount of suspicion by the pinkos — as reflected in the pieces here that deal with the fellow I call Harold the Committed, who has got it into his head that I am not a serious person. I have, of course, tried to be open with Harold the Committed about my own most deeply held political beliefs. "I am firmly committed to the proposition that whoever is in power is exceedingly silly, Hal the C," I told him. "And that goes for the opposition as well." Still, people like Harold always suspect that someone hired to make jokes (if "hired" is a word that can be applied to my situation) judges the events of the day — even disastrous events of the day — partly according to whether they might provide good material. People like Harold are right. Someone hired to make jokes is bound to view, say, some particularly loony decision of the Reagan Administration partly the way a dentist views tooth decay: it's a pity, but business wouldn't be nearly as good without it.

"How do I know what you really said to Harold the Committed?" the hardnose would ask. "Harold the Committed might not even exist. How do you expect anybody to know what's true in these pieces?"

At that point, I would be faced with the task of separating the real characters from the fictional ones — a somewhat awkward task for me, I'm afraid, because I'm not certain that in every case I can remember. I know I made up my Aunt Rosie, who wanted to offer her house as the site of the Nixon Presidential Library, and I definitely did not make up my Uncle Benny. After that, I get a little fuzzy. "It's all very complicated," I'd say.

But those hardnosed types are never satisfied. "Let's be specific," the reporter would say. "Is there really a wily and parsimonious Victor S. Navasky who pays you a century for each column?"

"That," I would reply in all honesty, "is a very embarrassing question."

*   *   *

I have fiddled a bit with a few of these columns, and in one or two cases I have made a switch in order. Otherwise they appear here as they did in *The Nation*. One piece appeared in the first issue of the reborn *Vanity Fair* rather than in *The Nation* simply because an editor of *Vanity Fair* happened to knock on the door about the time I was preparing a column that asked why I had not received a letter from the publisher inviting me to subscribe. That piece is entitled "Invitations" here, but around the house we refer to it as the *Nation* column I got paid for.

Damaged Goods

January 2, 1982
I HEARD on the morning news that some kidnappers
in the Bronx telephoned the wife of their victim with
a demand for $100,000 in ransom money, and she
talked them down to $30,000. The newscaster said the
story had a happy ending — the victim was returned
unharmed, the ransom money was recovered, the kidnappers were arrested — but all I could think of was
how the man must have felt when, back in the bosom
of his loving family at last, he discovered that his wife
had him on discount special. I suppose a lot of people
who heard the story took it as just one more indication
that New York City is getting to be one of those places,
like Bombay or Tijuana, where the price is always ne-
gotiable. They could probably imagine the victim's wife
standing in front of some huge counter, poking at her
husband the way she might poke at a cantaloupe, and
saying, "A hundred grand for that! The way it's going
soft around the sides already! You have the nerve to

· 6 ·

stand here and tell me that you are trying to charge one hundred thousand American dollars for *that!*"

Even a resident of the American Bombay, though, has to be disturbed at the prospect of having a loved one treat him the way she would treat an overripe cantaloupe. "What if I got kidnapped and they called demanding ransom money?" I asked my wife, Alice, after stewing over the Bronx caper for a couple of days. "I don't suppose you'd have any inclination to see if you could talk them into settling for thirty cents on the dollar, would you?"

"You're not going to get kidnapped," Alice said. "Why can't you just worry about high interest rates or acid rain or The Bomb, like normal people?"

As it happens, I didn't use to worry much about being kidnapped: I figured that kidnappers who were looking for good ransom prospects would automatically eliminate from consideration anyone publicly identified as an employee of Victor S. Navasky, the only magazine editor in New York who continues to maintain that columnists are exempt from the provisions of the minimum wage law. In fact, I wouldn't be surprised to hear that Navasky mentions that sort of thing to prospective employees when the discussion turns from salary to fringe benefits — a turn Navasky must make pretty abruptly, hoping that the jolt might loosen the prospect's grasp on the precise salary figure mentioned. Where another employer might mention medical plans or incentive bonuses, Navasky probably talks about what a relief it can be to be relatively free from the threat of kidnapping or the certainty of being solicited by the United Jewish Appeal or the complicated problems of tax shelters or any of the other inconveniences that must be faced daily by the prosperous.

After I heard the kidnapping story from the Bronx, though, it began to occur to me that the days when kidnappers limited their efforts to the better-known names of Manhattan café society may be over. It's possible that the sagging economy has driven kidnappers to the outer boroughs. I had to consider the possibility that some particularly desperate gang was staking out the garage in Brooklyn where I take my car to be repaired. If so, I'm in real danger: if a kidnapper tried to calculate my net worth by simply extrapolating from the amount of money I've poured into that wretched machine, he would figure me for eight or ten million dollars at the least.

All of which meant that I also had to consider the possibility that I might be the cantaloupe being discussed in a scene that flashed across my mind:

KIDNAPPER: Look, lady, even at eighty grand I'd barely come out on the deal myself. I mean, with the price of getaway cars these days and —
ALICE: You mean eighty thousand *before* we knock off the ten for softness around the sides, right?

"Don't get me wrong," I said to Alice. "Nobody could blame you for reminding the perpetrators that it's going to be impossible for this country to get inflation down to some manageable level unless people in every walk of life make some effort toward voluntary control of wages and prices."

"I've never understood why you don't get a hobby," Alice said.

Was it mere chance that she did not directly deny that she might ever consider me cut-rate merchandise? Was it really possible that she might respond to the dread call with a little dickering?

> KIDNAPPER: We got him, lady, and we want a hundred grand pronto.
> ALICE: (Long tactical silence)

"I suppose there's no reason to assume that just because someone happens to be your husband he's automatically worth the full sticker price," I said.

"Maybe you should get involved in some sort of volunteer work," she said. "Afternoons part-time at one of the thrift shops — something like that."

"Aside from some mileage on the odometer," I said, "I'm sure I have a few little faults that might be mentioned by someone interested in lowering the asking price just a little."

"You mean little faults like going on and on about some particularly silly subject?" Alice said.

"Well, I hadn't actually thought of that, as a matter of fact." Then I did think of it:

> KIDNAPPER: Lady, he's driving us batty with all this talk about full sticker price.
> ALICE: Why don't we talk again tomorrow, after you've had a chance to get to know him a little better.

"Of course, adding that to some softness around the sides," Alice said. "Plus some mileage — quite a bit of mileage, really — on the odometer —"

"I don't think it's necessary to plan it all in detail," I said. "It's really very unlikely."

"You're right," Alice said. "And if the need to decide whether you're worth top dollar ever does come up, I can just ask the advice of Victor S. Navasky."

Small Leaks

October 31, 1981

THE TIP I GOT was this: the Reagans decided against attending Anwar el-Sadat's funeral not because of the security considerations mentioned by the White House press office but because Mrs. Reagan's hairdresser had warned that the Cairo humidity might, in his words, "frizz the hair into a state I simply can't be responsible for." Ever since I broke the story that Mrs. Reagan was called Bubbles in high school, I seem to be the reporter people call whenever they want to unload some mean-minded little leak about the First Family. Ironically, what I really want to do is to grapple with the big issues, but nobody ever calls me with big-issue leaks. The sort of thing I spend my time checking out is whether Mrs. Reagan really tried to get the President to fire the Secretary of Housing and Urban Development because he clashed with the new rug in the Cabinet room. It's pretty easy to get typed in this business. It wouldn't surprise me to hear that every time

Woodward or Bernstein gets himself really wrapped up in reporting a piece on farm price supports or the reorganization of the Department of Forestry, someone calls with a tip about some President committing a felony.

I was particularly disappointed because I thought the Sadat funeral would result in a lot of important foreign policy leaks — particularly after it was announced that Richard Nixon's parole officer was going to allow him to go along as one of the official American representatives. I expected someone to call and say, "Reagan's planning to send Billy Sol Estes to Manila as our representative at the Martial Law Celebrations. Check it out."

"Why don't you ever call one of the big-issue columnists with this kind of thing?" I asked the hair-frizz leaker.

"I tried," he said. "They've all got unlisted numbers."

No matter what is written these days about the romance of investigative reporting, I can tell you that it's no fun checking out the sort of leaks I get ("Let me get this straight now: You're saying, for the record, that the story couldn't be true because in high humidity Mrs. Reagan's hair tends not to frizz but to go limp?"). No sooner had I decided that the hair-frizz story was untrue — the limp-hair denial checked out with some of my sources on the Coast — than the telephone rang again. I knew it was another small-bore leaker.

"Are you the one workin' the hair-frizz story?" a rough voice asked.

"Well, yes, although I have to say that it's really not my sort of —"

"While you're at it, you might check out another angle," the caller said.

"Some national security scandal?" I asked hopefully.

"In a manner of speaking," the voice said. "Let's put it this way: Do you think Mrs. Reagan's hairdresser should be getting Secret Service protection?"

"Is he really getting Secret Service protection?"

"Check it out," the voice said.

"Wait! Don't hang up," I said. "I'd like to talk to you about some big issues."

"You'll hear from me," the voice said. "I'll be phoning in the morning to let you know about how the price of Mrs. Reagan's new ball gown compares with the gross national product of Chad."

I started checking out the Secret Service tip ("Yes, I know you're busy, but could you just see if one of the people sitting under a dryer near where Mister Marc is working looks like he went to Georgetown and is carrying a gun?"). I was still checking my beauty parlor sources when I noticed that a lot of stories about the Reagans' extravagance were beginning to appear — some of them written by people who normally go in for the big issues. I saw a few stories about the cost of the new White House china. I saw some stories about the President's one-thousand-dollar cowboy boots. Then Hugh Sidey, coming to the First Family's defense in his *Time* column, revealed that some of the President's one-thousand-dollar suits were ten years old — leaving the implication that a President like Richard Nixon would have long ago given such rags to the thrift shop and taken a $2800 tax write-off on each suit. Could it be that Sidey asked his best White House source for permission to sit in on a Middle East strategy session and was instead given a tour of Reagan's closet? ("This double vent was never used by Beverly Hills tailors after 1974, Hugh. You can check it out.")

I realized that the issue gap was closing. Some important Washington reporter was probably being called that moment by a White House counter-tipster with deep background dope on the cost of Mrs. Reagan's ball gown ("I happen to know that it's several hundred dollars below the poverty-line annual income for a family of four"). Some syndicated columnist with strong ties to the Administration would soon be writing a column in defense of giving Mrs. Reagan's hairdresser Secret Service protection ("Although those who have not seen the cables do not seem to realize it, the Soviets are perfectly capable of pressuring a hairdresser into inserting one of those little Japanese listening devices in the First Lady's follicles"). I waited for the next telephone call with a new sense of importance: my leaks were as big as anyone's.

Navasky as Male Model

———

November 21, 1981

THUMBING THROUGH the *New York Times Magazine* one Sunday, noticing that more and more designers like Ralph Lauren and Bill Blass and Oscar de la Renta are appearing in advertisements for their own brands of clothing, I was struck so suddenly with an inspiration that I blurted it out to my wife, Alice: "Victor S. Navasky should appear in ads for *The Nation*," I said. "Standing with his foot on the corral fence, next to one of those blond models who look like they're too sophisticated to eat dinner."

"Victor!" Alice said. "In *that* suit?"

"He wouldn't be peddling shmatas," I said. "We're talking about a journal of opinion here. Journalists are supposed to be a bit seedy, and you have to admit that Navasky is very opinionated looking. He looks like he holds a number of opinions that other people gave up a long time ago."

"If this is another plot to embarrass Victor just because you think he's underpaying you, I want you to forget it immediately," Alice said. "It's not his fault he doesn't look like a male model."

"But that's just the point," I said. "Neither do those designers. Does Ralph Lauren strike you as someone who used to be a lifeguard?"

"Well, no," Alice acknowledged. "In fact, it's always seemed to me that Oscar de la Renta looks like a ruffle with legs."

"As it happens, Victor S. Navasky has an athletic past — he was on the basketball team at Elisabeth Irwin High School," I said, repeating an old and unconvincing Navasky claim that I figured I could pass off as true because Alice has never seen him play basketball. Years ago, Navasky and I both played in a weekly Sunday morning basketball game at the Gansevoort Street Playground in the West Village, but Alice had always declined my invitations to attend.

"I don't know much about basketball," she used to say, "and I'm afraid I'll laugh at the wrong time."

"It isn't meant to be funny at all," I would tell her — another statement I thought I might get away with because she had never seen Navasky play.

Navasky was dreadful. I don't mean he received no awards at the annual banquet we held in the spring at the Paradise Inn of the Green Olive Tree, on Forty-first Street. We had a number of awards that had nothing to do with skill — Most Improved Jewish Player, for instance, and the Richard Nixon Award for the Most

Specious Out-of-Bounds Argument. His playing was such, though, that the only reason the rest of us agreed among ourselves to quit scoffing at his story of having played on the high school basketball team was to prevent him from embarrassing his family and friends by wearing his letter sweater to dinner parties.

Being unusually charitable about such matters, I finally managed to devise a theory that might explain how an American high school could have had Victor S. Navasky as a member of its basketball team — a theory based on the assumption that Elisabeth Irwin, a Greenwich Village school with a progressive reputation, must have been full of children from left-wing families. It seems possible to me that in order to avoid sectarian disputes at PTA meetings, the basketball coach might have tried to give the teams a fair balance of all sorts of players — a few Trotskyites, a couple of Stalinist forwards, a Schachtmanite with a passable jump shot, maybe an energetic guard who couldn't hit the basket but had a grandfather who had been a Left S.R. in the old country. Navasky, I figured, must have been editing the Elisabeth Irwin newspaper, charging his writers their lunch money for the opportunity of getting into print, and he was put on the second five as the Token Exploiter.

"How about a campus scene?" I said to Alice the next day. "Navasky's in a sweater — not his E.I. letter sweater but one of those gigantic Irish fisherman's sweaters that male models can wear to Sunday brunch in a steam-heated New York apartment once they've had their sweat glands surgically removed. He's reading *The Nation*. His foot's on a corral fence — because there happens to be a corral on this campus — and he's so engrossed he doesn't notice that all of these dynamite coeds are staring at him with a desperate longing. Some of them have long, straight hair, so they look a little left-wing, except for being such knockouts."

"I can't believe you're doing this," Alice said.

"Or maybe Navasky's on a beach," I said. "In gauzy color. He's wearing one of those alligator polo shirts, except it's got a peace sign or a Red Star or something where the alligator's supposed to be. He's reading *The Nation*, and so are all of these marvelous-looking people on the beach — everyone but the lifeguard, this wonky little guy who looks something like Ralph Lauren."

"I think you're being awful," Alice said. "You can't compare Victor to some dress designer. He's a serious person, except for that suit."

"But dress designers are not the only people appearing in their own ads now," I said. "What about Frank Perdue — with all those ads about how it takes a tough man to produce a tender chicken? Is that your idea of a glamour puss? What about that Carvel ice cream guy with the voice they make political prisoners in Central America listen to until they agree to confess to being in the pay of the Kremlin? It's just that I prefer to envision Navasky in an Irish fisherman's sweater."

"I won't have Victor discussed as if he were a ruffle," Alice said.

"Maybe you're right," I said. "We could do a sort of Perdue-style ad for *The Nation*. There's Navasky, dressed up like Edward Arnold playing the big industrialist in one of those 1940s movies, and writers are slaving away all around him — all of them dressed in dismal clothes and needing haircuts and looking undernourished."

"I don't see the point," Alice said.

"The caption, of course: 'It Takes a Real Exploiter of the Workers to Run a Left-Wing Magazine.' "

Voodoo Economics:
An Eyewitness Account

February 13, 1982

"I DON'T LIKE the sound of those drums, dear," Edgar said. "I think we should go back to the hotel."

Their guide turned to face them. "You be coming with me, kind mister," he said. "You be seeing real voodoo economics ritual. No touristy stuff. Plenty supply side." The guide nudged Edgar in the ribs with his elbow, and said in a softer voice, "You be seeing swollen bureaucracy turned into nude federalism, my mister."

"You mean *New* Federalism," Edgar said.

"Don't quibble, dear," Emily said, gesturing for the guide to continue down the winding dirt path they were following. "You can't just sit in the hotel all day reading John Kenneth Galbraith."

The guide continued toward a thick grove of trees — gnarled trees of surpassing weirdness, their limbs heavy with ticker tape.

"I simply don't like those drums," Edgar said. "It sounds like someone's beating the hustings. And listen to that chant!"

In the distance, the sound of voices grew louder and louder. "Voo-doo, voo-doo — trickle, trickle, trickle, trickle," the voices droned in a rhythmic chant. "Voo-doo, voo-doo — trickle, trickle, trickle, trickle."

"Isn't this all simply fascinating?" Emily said, picking her way around a pile of discarded water and sewer grants. "I hope the ceremony's not too bloody, though. Thelma and Harry said that when they went last year the sorceress just used some leftovers from the hot-lunch program for the gris-gris. Some people at their hotel said they heard she could change two helpings of broccoli into an aircraft carrier."

"Voo-doo, voo-doo — trickle, trickle, trickle, trickle," the voices chanted. "Voo-doo, voo-doo — trickle, trickle, trickle, trickle."

"I don't like it, I tell you," Edgar said. "It gives me the creeps. And why does our guide look so much like an oil company lobbyist?"

The guide turned to face them on the path, his eyes darting from side to side, his lips curled in a slight smile. "You be seeing real stuff, my fine sir," he said. "You be seeing too, my kind young lady. Magic! White magic! Lily White Magic! You be seeing less make more, and machine tools depreciate lightning fast before your eyes, quick-quick."

"But what's that awful smell?" Edgar asked.

The guide began to cackle. "We be cooking the

figures, mister," he said, shaking with mirth and rubbing his hands together. "Heh, heh, heh, heh. We be cooking hell out of the figures. Heh, heh, heh, heh, heh."

They had reached a clearing in the grove of trees, and the chant now seemed nearly deafening. "Voo-doo, voo-doo — trickle, trickle, trickle, trickle. Voo-doo, voo-doo — trickle, trickle, trickle, trickle."

"You be seeing now, kind mister," the guide said. "You be seeing now poor folk bounce on safety nets. You be seeing rich folk bounce on poor folk. You be seeing this too, my kind young lady."

The chanters had reached the clearing. They were wearing hooded robes of polyester. As they stood at the edge of the clearing, their chant changed: "Two, four, six, eight — what shall we depreciate?" Then one of the robed figures stepped out from the chorus, slowly walked toward the center of the clearing, violently twisted back in his own tracks at a grotesque angle, and fell, writhing, to the ground — presumably having displaced a vertebra or perhaps even broken his back. Edgar and Emily watched in horror as one chanter after another followed the bizarre ritual.

"They be walking the Laffer curve, kind young lady," the guide said, noticing the look of distress on Emily's face.

"Those poor men!" Emily cried.

"Not for you being worried, kind miss," the guide said. "They be suffering only short-term displacement."

"I'm not so sure I like this," Emily whispered to Edgar. "Maybe we should just go back to that recreation area at the hotel and try to balance the budget on the backs of some American taxpayers. Thelma says it's not that hard once you get the hang of it, except she kept slipping off the rich ones."

Just then, a new group of chanters entered the clearing, moving in a sort of jazz rhythm. Gyrating in a way that made Emily blush, they shouted, "Trickle down, trickle down — let's go to town and trickle down!"

"I'd like to go now, Edgar," Emily said, but at that moment the voodoo sorceress appeared.

"There she is!" Edgar said.

"That be her, nice people," the guide said. "Now you be seeing her stick pins into neo-Keynesian dollies, kind missus."

"Why is she wearing an Adolfo gown?" Emily asked.

"You be watching, good people," the guide said. "She be sacrificing chicken and giving the back and gizzard to poor folk on strictly volunteer basis."

The chorus now began hauling some sort of idol on wheels into the clearing.

"It's a Trojan horse," Edgar said.

"There be the chicken now, kind mister," the guide said.

"That's no chicken; that's a Trojan horse," Emily said, as the sorceress slit open the belly of the horse and tax breaks for the rich began to pour out.

"Nice fat chicken it be," the guide said. "Lucky poor be getting nice fat gizzard."

"Let's get out of here, Edgar!" Emily said.

"Furthermore," the guide continued, "a deregulated oil and natural-gas industry assures all Americans a dependable energy supply within the framework of traditional American free enterprise."

"Jesus Christ!" Edgar said. "He *is* an oil company lobbyist!" Edgar grabbed Emily's hand, and they scrambled toward the path.

"It be nice chicken," the guide shouted after them, having quickly fallen back into his role. "Voodoo be bringing chicken in every pot, two cars in every garage."

famous professional basketball player telling kids that it isn't cool to smoke marijuana. I don't remember which famous professional basketball player it was: I wasn't concentrating very well because I was irritated at having the cartoons interrupted. Even without concentrating very well, I was able to get the impression from the famous professional basketball player that if you smoke a lot of marijuana you won't be able to sink a twenty-five-foot jump shot with any consistency. I liked that commercial too. It's true that I don't smoke marijuana and I still can't seem to sink a jump shot, but the reason for that, I finally decided several years ago, is that I must have a deeply repressed clubfoot.

About the time I saw the commercial with the famous basketball player, I read that Edward I. Koch, the Municipal Yenta, has devised another strategy for dealing with spray-paint graffiti in the subways. The mayor is dropping his get-tough policy in favor of a campaign to have celebrities persuade teen-agers that painting graffiti in the subways is not cool. I suppose there will be subway ads, like the ads that feature celebrities urging us to blow the rent money on Off-Track Betting. I don't know what the mayor plans to do about the problem of having the anti-graffiti ads covered with graffiti, but I like the idea anyway. I only hope that the abandonment of the get-tough policy on graffiti painters doesn't mean that the mayor is dropping my suggestion that any academic or literary hustler caught writing that graffiti is a fascinating expression of artistic and cultural creativity be sprayed magenta and left without grants for a year, sentences to be served consecutively.

My only quibble with the trend toward what is now being called "moral suasion" is that I don't think teenagers are the only people who could do with a bit of suasing. Why aren't there any moral suasion commercials, for instance, that feature celebrities telling middle-aged people that snorting cocaine is not cool? The sort of commercial I have in mind would consist of a conversation between Paul Newman and Robert Redford. They would be in their jeans. Not designer jeans. Jeans.

"Melvin Schmeckle offered me some coke on the set today," Bob would say.

Paul wouldn't say anything for a while. Then he'd say, "It figures." Then he wouldn't say anything for a while.

Then Bob would say, "It just confirms what I've always said about who snorts cocaine: the sort of Hollywood screen writer who wears his shirt unbuttoned and couldn't get dates in high school."

Paul nods, and gives his knowing smile. Paul has a very knowing smile. He nods for a long time, and keeps smiling his knowing smile. This is a long commercial.

Bob nods himself. Then he says, "C.P.A.s who walk like a duck." Bob does a little imitation of a guy snorting cocaine while walking like a duck.

Paul starts to laugh, and says, "Orthodontists with gold chains."

"Pear-shaped guys wearing designer jeans and pinkie rings," Bob says.

Paul tries to reply, but he's laughing too hard. As the camera fades out, Bob continues to list the sort of middle-aged people who snort cocaine, while Paul, convulsed with laughter, holds up his hand in a request for mercy.

"The guy who was the corresponding secretary of the stamp club," Bob says. "Stockbrokers who take disco lessons . . . hip estate-planners . . ."

I hadn't thought about the possibility of using moral suasion commercials as an instrument of foreign policy until I saw a television interview with the Assistant Secretary of State for Human Rights and Humanitarian Affairs. He said that when it comes to human rights problems in friendly countries, we ought to use quiet persuasion instead of getting all het up, the way the Carter people did. From what he said, I guess there are American ambassadors all over South America telling the general in charge things like, "You know, we'd sure think a lot higher of you, general, if you'd quit making so many folks disappear." The trouble is that the ambassadors aren't celebrities. What sort of moral suasion can you expect to get out of someone who probably only last year was a car dealer in Southern California?

I figure what the State Department needs is a series of commercials with Patti LuPone, in her strapless "Evita" gown. They could run on one of those blue-movie cable channels, to reach the diplomatic crowd. "I like strong men," Patti would say. "Also strongmen." She is, of course, smiling her knowing smile. Talk about a knowing smile! I have no idea what Patti LuPone knows, but it must be even more than Paul Newman knows.

"I met a strongman I thought I was going to like," Patti says. "I liked his cars. I liked his Swiss bank account." Patti suddenly looks very serious. "Then I heard that he closes newspapers and runs torture chambers and makes people disappear," she says. She shakes her head sadly. "And to think," she says, "for a moment there, I thought he was a cool guy."

The Gout:
A Reassessment

March 27, 1982

I SUPPOSE you've heard by now that I had the gout. Everybody seems to know. No, I don't want to hear about your grandfather's gout. With the possible exception of your grandmother, nobody is less interested in hearing about your grandfather than I am. No, the gout does not make people ill tempered. I have nothing against your grandfather — although I must admit that even before the onset of my own affliction, stories concerning the inflammation of his joints would not have been high on my list of compelling narratives. The reason I'm adamant right now about not wanting to discuss your grandfather is that the association of the gout with grandfathers — particularly grandfathers who look like Charles Laughton — is symptomatic of a view of gout that we gout sufferers consider a very large pain in the foot.

Don't deny it. Charles Laughton is precisely the sort

of person you had in mind. I know that from the smile Alice had on her face when she guessed that I might have the gout — after having dismissed, without anything approaching a scientific inquiry, my theory that I might be suffering from the effects of a tarantula bite. I heard that Charles Laughton echo in the voice of my doctor, who took one look at my foot and said, "Looks like a touch of the gout, old boy." I know the picture he had in his mind: some bloated old Tory sunk into a leather armchair in a musty gentlemen's club, resting one foot on a gout-stool as he tries to maneuver the other foot into position to kick at a passing waiter. Don't tell me: you were just about to say that the gout is the disease of the rich and distinguished. I know what you really mean. You really mean that people who have the gout are rich enough to guzzle vintage port and distinguished by a tendency to let cigar ashes dribble onto their vests as they doze off in the middle of the afternoon. Don't deny it.

Your attitude is the reason I decided that there had to be a serious effort to re-educate the public on the subject of the gout — which, of course, is not the name our affliction will go by once the re-education effort is in high gear.

"We need to come up with a new name," I told Alice. "Maybe something that sounds breezy, like the names they use these days for new brands of cigarettes."

"How about Glutton's Syndrome?" Alice said.

I explained to her that according to modern medical theory gout is more likely to have to do with heredity than with diet — although just to be safe I have always steered clear of mung beans and broccoli. Then it occurred to me that we might name the disease after one or another of its most renowned sufferers, such as Dr. Samuel Johnson — the eighteenth-century literary figure, not the oral surgeon.

"What about calling it Johnson's Disease?" I asked.

"That's a dumb name," she said. "People will think it's named after Lyndon Johnson. They'll think the symptoms include a mad compulsion to bomb Orientals."

Dumb! I wasn't going to bring this up, but, as it happens, studies suggest a correlation between Dr. Johnson's Disease (formerly gout) and high intelligence. Name three dummies who have ever had Dr. Johnson's Disease. See! The re-education campaign is in high gear already.

In planning the campaign, I got off on the wrong foot — a phrase, I must say, that still makes me wince, even though some little pills the doctor gave me cleared up my symptoms (or coincided with the gradual neutralizing of the tarantula venom I had absorbed). The false association of gout with the Blimps had made me obsessed with distinguishing the sort of people who actually do get Dr. Johnson's Disease (Galileo, for instance, and Richard the Lion-Hearted) from the sort of people who don't. Roy Cohn, the New York bar's best-known limousine-chaser, had just thrown the annual birthday celebration that I have always thought of as the Foxhole Party, since it brings together all of the most prominent people you wouldn't want to have in the next foxhole, and I became preoccupied with proving that the sort of people who contract Dr. Johnson's Disease would not be in attendance. As a public service, the *Soho News*, of blessed memory, usually had a reporter on hand at the Foxhole Party to note the names of guests as they arrived — the way the FBI stations someone at the cemetery to check out the mourners at a mob funeral — and I was poring over the list when Alice told me I was wasting my time trying to prove that no sufferer of Dr. Johnson's Disease would attend a party held at a disco.

"That little jig that Hitler danced when he heard about the fall of France would have been impossible for a man with Dr. Johnson's Disease," I informed her.

"I think you need professional help," she said.

I tried to get some from a friend in the public relations business. He suggested that we build a campaign around television commercials featuring Bruce Jenner, the decathlon champion, and have as our first big fund-raiser a benefit performance of that new film *I'm Dancing as Fast as I Can*. The commercials would show Jenner just barely outrunning and outjumping some beach-boy type, and would then cut to the locker room, where Jenner says to the beach boy, "Hey, you're not bad for a guy with the gout."

"We call it Dr. Johnson's Disease, or D.J.D., these days, Bruce," the beach boy says, with diction that makes it obvious he is not a beach boy but maybe an associate professor of classics. "And with proper medication, people who suffer from it can lead full and productive lives."

You can be assured that I rejected that campaign out of hand. I don't want people to think that those of us who have D.J.D. do not suffer. We want respect, sure, but not at the cost of losing sympathy. D.J.D. hurts. Sometimes I had to keep my foot up on a stool. Sometimes I got, well, out of sorts, which you would get too if your foot hurt and you weren't allowed any wine as long as you were taking little pills. Sometimes what bothered me most about my foot hurting was that I couldn't use it to drop-kick a cat. Sometimes the medication made me doze off. You suspected as much, didn't you? Don't deny it.

Pinko Problems

April 17, 1982
I'VE BEEN WORRIED lately about the possibility that
The Nation is getting to be known around the country
for being a bit pinko. I was born and brought up in
Kansas City, and I'm not really keen on the folks at
home getting the impression that I work for a left-wing
sheet. They know I do a column for *The Nation*, of
course — my mother told them — but most of them
have not inquired deeply into *The Nation*'s politics,
perhaps because my mother has been sort of letting on
that it's a tennis magazine. She has been able to get
away with that so far because *The Nation* is not cir-
culated widely in Kansas City: in the greater Kansas
City area, it goes weekly to three librarians and an un-
reconstructed old anarcho-syndicalist who moved to
town after his release from the federal prison at Leavenworth in 1927 and set up practice as a crank. Lately,
though, I've had reason to worry that *The Nation*'s
political views may be revealed in the press.

· 3 5 ·

My concern is not based on any notion that the people back home would react to this revelation by ostracizing my mother for having given birth to a Commie rat. Folks in the Midwest try to be nice. What I'm worried about is this: People in Kansas City will assume that no one would write a column for a pinko rag if he could write a column for a respectable periodical. They might even assume that payment for a column in a pinko rag would be the sort of money people in Kansas City associate with the summer retainer for the boy who mows the lawn. They could even go to the library — or to the home of the crank, who holds on to back issues in case they're needed for reference in sectarian disputes — and look through my columns until they find the one that revealed the luncheon negotiations in which I asked the editor of *The Nation*, one Victor S. Navasky, what he intended to pay for each of these columns and he replied, "Somewhere in the high two figures." Then the people at home, realizing that I had struggled for years in New York only to end up writing a column in a pinko rag for lawn-mowing wages, would spend a lot of time comforting my mother whenever they ran into her at the supermarket. ("There, there. Don't you worry one bit. Things have a way of working themselves out.") My mom's pretty tough, but tougher people have broken under the burden of Midwestern comforting.

Without wanting to name names, I blame all of this on Victor S. Navasky. During the aforementioned luncheon negotiations, he said nothing that would have led me to think that *The Nation* had political views I might find embarrassing. In fact, he sort of let on that it was a tennis magazine. The only reference he made to anybody who could be considered even marginally pinko was when he told me that he had reason to believe that Warren Beatty was keeping his eye on *The Nation* and might snatch up the movie rights to just about any piece for $200,000 plus 5 percent of the gross. "Always get points on the gross, never on the net," I remember Navasky saying as I dealt with the check.

When Navasky provoked a public controversy by attacking a book on the Hiss case from a position that might have been described as somewhat left of center, I tried to be understanding. I figured that Navasky was trying to pump up circulation because he lacked some of the financial resources that most people who edit journals of opinion have. Traditionally, people who run such magazines manage financially because they have a wife rich enough to have bought them the magazine in the first place. It's a good arrangement, because an editor who has his own forum for pontificating to the public every week may tend to get a bit pompous around the house, and it helps if his wife is in a position to say, "Get off your high horse, Harry, or I'll take your little magazine away from you and give it to the cook." I haven't made any detailed investigation into the finances of Navasky's wife, but it stands to reason that if she had the wherewithal to acquire entire magazines she would by now have bought him a new suit.

There is no excuse, though, for Navasky's latest caper, particularly after I had specifically said to him only last year, "I don't care what your politics are, Navasky, but I hope you'll have the good taste to keep them to yourself." A couple of months ago, around the time Susan Sontag charged in her Town Hall speech that left-wing journals had never really faced up to the basic evil of the Soviet regime, *The Nation* began advertising a tour it was co-sponsoring — a "Cruise up the Volga." The other co-sponsors were outfits with names like National Council of American-Soviet Friendship. The advertised attractions included a visit to Lenin's birthplace. I suppose some long-buried smidgen of restraint kept Navasky from simply headlining the ad "Pinko Tours Inc. Offers a Once-in-a-Lifetime Opportunity to Fellow Travelers." Didn't he know he would be attacked by *The New Republic*? Didn't he know that he would provoke an argument about the possibility that what *Nation* tourists need to examine is not the GUM department store but the loony bins where dissidents are stashed? Didn't he know this sort of thing could get back to Kansas City?

I implored Navasky to cut his losses by explaining the tour in humanitarian terms. Where, after all, are old Commies supposed to go for their vacations — Palm Springs?

"The tour is oversubscribed," he said.

I could see that he was getting defensive. He had the look I noticed when I asked him if it was really true that two elderly Wobbly copyreaders at *The Nation* had been told that their salaries were still being diverted straight into a defense fund for Big Bill Haywood. I knew that in his mood he might even launch some preventive strikes — maybe write an editorial suggesting that *Commentary* give its readers a New York tour that included the Brooklyn street where Norman Podhoretz was first taunted by black kids and the office where Daniel Bell got his first government grant.

"I'm going," I said.

"To Russia?" he asked.

"To call my mother," I said.

The Mailbag

———

May 29, 1982

SIR: I DON'T KNOW who to believe anymore. First the *Washington Post* and the *New York Times Magazine* have to admit that they ran phony stories; now Ann Landers and Abigail Van Buren have both been caught recycling used letters from secondhand kvetches. It occurs to me that you may be making up quotations and letters yourself and that may explain why your column has always sounded a little — if you'll forgive me for saying so — cockamamie. Can I trust you? Please try to be truthful in your response.

R.F.G., Pelham, N.Y.

Trust me. I know some misunderstanding might have been caused by my admitting in public print recently that the editor of The Nation, *one Victor S. Navasky, once asked me whether a certain quotation I had attributed to John Foster Dulles ("You can't fool*

· 4 0 ·

all of the people all of the time, but you might as well give it your best shot") was authentic, and I answered, "At these rates, you can't always expect real quotes." However, everyone involved understood that to be a negotiating tactic rather than an admission of guilt. As to concocting letters, I can assure you that yours is the first.

Sir: Ten years ago, I wrote a letter to Ann Landers about my husband, who thought he was Katharine Hepburn. I signed it with a pseudonym ("Concerned"), but everyone knew it was me, of course, because I am the only Swedenborgian in Luke's Crossing, Montana. Miss Landers gave me what I thought was sensible advice ("Tell him his slip is showing"). Recently, though, she reprinted the letter as if it had just been sent, and, as it happens, I have a different husband now. He's very upset because he thinks he's Wallace Beery. If Abigail Van Buren prints it, can I sue?

R.V.M., Luke's Crossing, Mont.

Pull up your socks.

Sir: Is it true that employees of *The Nation* are forced to sell flowers and candy in airports and turn the proceeds over to Victor S. Navasky?

G.B., Dayton, Ohio

Not exactly.

Sir: I have been a loyal subscriber to *The Nation* for forty-five years, and I simply can't imagine what possessed them to begin running a column by a bubblehead such as yourself. Where are your politics, young man? Why don't you ever write about the Scottsboro Boys? What's your position on the withering away of the state?

S.A.S., Boston, Mass.

I was once intensely political. I had a position on everything. If something new came up, I'd get a position on it by the end of that week at the latest. Then a lot of new countries came into being, and a political person had to have a position on every one of them. One day, someone said to me, "I don't think much of your position on Guinea."

"My position on Guinea is impeccable," I said. By chance, I had that very morning taken out my position on Guinea and tidied it up a bit. "What is your objection to my position on Guinea?" I thought about calling him a crypto-fascist pig straight off, but I decided to keep that card up my sleeve.

"To start with, you don't have it in the right continent," he said. "It's in Africa."

"Well, no wonder some people thought that the Indonesian territorial claims were historically dubious," I said. "Still, as a Third World country, Indonesia —"

"That's New Guinea," he said.

"Is it possible we're talking about Ghana?" I said. "Or maybe British Guiana?"

"There isn't any British Guiana," he said. *"It's Guyana now. What's your position on Guyana?"*

"I'd rather not say," I told him.

I tried to catch up, of course, but I found that I no longer had time to do the dishes, and at the office I was falling behind in my work. Finally, I decided I could no longer be political. I kept a position on British unilateral disarmament, as a sort of souvenir, but nobody ever asks me about it — which is a shame, because it's impeccable.

Sir: Did Victor S. Navasky name names?

S.F., Kansas City, Mo.

It's all very complicated.

Sir: Don't you think CBS should have allowed the White House equal time to reply to that Bill Moyers program about three families that slipped through the social safety net? How can the press expect people to take it seriously when the networks just tell one side of the story and Ann Landers and Abigail Van Buren both keep running the same letter about some wacko in Montana who still thinks he's Katharine Hepburn?

M.N.V., Chicago, Ill.

The President's advisers differed as to how to reply. Some thought the reply should be an upbeat program showing three millionaires who were happy as clams and about to leave for extended vacations on the Con-

tinent, where they intended to depreciate Luxembourg. The hard-liners wanted to show that the parents involved were acting irresponsibly, since it was obvious that children as skinny and undernourished as theirs would slip through any net. The debate finally had to be settled by the President himself, and the program CBS rejected was to show a welfare chiseler driving to the supermarket in a Cadillac, buying vodka with food stamps, and giving birth to a child at the checkout counter just to qualify for Aid to Families with Dependent Children and the Wednesday coupon special.

Sir: Who said, "You can't fool all of the people all of the time, but you might as well give it your best shot"?

L.V., Troy, N.Y.

John Foster Dulles.

· 4 4 ·

Neediest Case

June 19, 1982

NO, I AM NOT one of those fickle bleeding hearts who take up the cause of some oppressed or needy person for a while and then lose interest when a more dashing wreck comes along. A year after I first discussed his case — a year after I identified him as the citizen Ronald Reagan might have had in mind when he used the phrase "truly needy" — I am still concerned about Philip Caldwell, the chairman of the Ford Motor Company, who in 1980 got no incentive bonus at all.

Don't think I've lacked opportunities to move along to the next cause. The pressure has been particularly strong from a politically intense acquaintance of mine who is known as Harold the Committed. A couple of months ago, for instance, Harold the Committed told me that I seemed insufficiently concerned about the prospect of nuclear annihilation.

"I've got other fish to fry, Harold," I said.

· 4 5 ·

"I don't believe you understand the gravity of the situation," Harold the Committed said. "Man now has the capacity to destroy himself and all future generations as well."

"Not if he works for Ford he doesn't," I said. "They don't seem to have a capacity for much of anything over there except losing money, Harold. They lost a billion and a half in 1980, and they took it out on Phil Caldwell."

Of course, Harold the Committed had considered it a bit quirky of me to take up Philip Caldwell's case in the first place. Even last year, though, I knew that Ronald Reagan must have had some corporation executive in mind when he talked about people who are truly needy, because he tends to talk about corporation executives whenever the conversation turns to suffering. When he tells those stories about some can-do American corporate manager being harassed by petty bureaucrats from OSHA and the Fair Employment Practices Commission and the District Attorney's office, I always have a vision of a fine running back being gang-tackled by a horde of midgets.

I learned of the Caldwell case a year ago through *Business Week*'s annual survey of executive compensation, always a good guide to the plight of the oppressed. Yes, it was clear from the figures in the survey that even without an incentive bonus Caldwell made $400,000 in 1980. Yes, I know now that if he was let in on some of the tax shelters that William French Smith, the Attorney General, knows about — one of those oil deals where any drilling done between Lafayette and Lake Charles entitles you to write off the cost of the Louisiana Purchase — he got to keep about $425,-000 of that. Yes, I do sometimes wonder if all of those welfare chiselers the President is always talking about would offend him less if they simply sheltered their relief checks and depreciated their government-surplus cheese.

Still, I couldn't help being concerned about Phil Caldwell, out there in Detroit with no incentive bonus. I could see him getting home from the office after a long day and having his wife say, as she handed him his martini, "Phil, little Johnny came home from school crying today. The other little boys told him that his daddy didn't have any incentive."

Naturally, I was a bit anxious this spring as I waited for *Business Week*'s survey of executive compensation for 1981 to appear on the stands. I wondered how things had gone for Phil Caldwell, given the recession and unemployment and the unfortunate matter of Ford's having lost another billion. The headline *Business Week* put on the survey gave some reason to believe that Caldwell's lot had improved: "No Sign of Recession in Pay at the Top." Executive compensation had gone up almost 16 percent in 1981, *Business Week* said, and a lot of executives were raking in a new goody called "incentive stock options." By the terms of the Reagan tax law, the taxes on the profits from an "incentive stock option" can be deferred and then paid at the capital gains rate of 20 percent — the sort of deal, it seems to me, that might summon up incentive in a petty bureaucrat. *Business Week* listed twenty-five executives who managed to make more than $1.5 million in 1981 despite all the bureaucrats pulling on their coattails and gnawing at their ankles. One of them, the executive vice-president for operations of Schlumbèrger, walked away with $5,658,000 even though the company he works for sounded to me like some sort of sausage factory.

I turned to the automotive section. The first thing I noticed was that Philip Caldwell got a raise in base salary to $440,000 last year — which, I'll admit, isn't really bad, particularly if he spent part of the year cozying up to William French Smith so he could get in on some of the Depreciator General's tax shelters. I suppose they had to give him a raise in base salary. How else would they reward him for the effort he has made persuading the workers to take what amounts to a pay cut? I looked at the incentive bonus column. In 1981 Philip Caldwell received no incentive bonus.

Just then, Harold the Committed dropped by to see if I would help him gather names for a petition against cuts in social services for the elderly.

"I still have this case in Detroit, Hal the C," I said. "Philip Caldwell got no incentive bonus at all for 1981, even though I have every reason to believe he was going flat-out all year long."

"But Caldwell made four hundred and forty thousand last year," Harold the Committed said.

"Think of how he must feel when he reads that some guy made five and a half million for turning out bratwurst," I said. "What if he loses his incentive altogether? After all, what separates people like Phil Caldwell from welfare chiselers and petty bureaucrats is incentive — that and the four hundred and forty grand."

Oratory of the Islands

July 10, 1982

I WASN'T QUITE SURE what J. Peter Grace meant when he said that he had made an "oratorical mistake" by describing the food stamp program in New York as "basically a Puerto Rican program." Mistake, sure, but what's so oratorical about "basically a Puerto Rican program"? Compared with, say, "Give me liberty or give me death!" it doesn't strike me as the sort of thing that brings them out of their seats.

I didn't have any trouble seeing how the mistake might have been made. Grace, who earned $1,809,882 last year (including a $1 million "special bonus") as chairman of W. R. Grace & Co., is not on food stamps and is not Puerto Rican; he simply extrapolated too far from his own situation. The mistake may even have originated with the officials who were assigned to brief Grace when he began chairing a commission of a hundred corporation executives asked by Ronald Reagan to recommend cuts in government operation costs:

· 50 ·

if the briefers had explained to Grace that food stamps could be considered the Puerto Ricans' "special bonus," he presumably would not have brought the subject up in the first place. Once he did, of course, Puerto Ricans became upset, and the Administration was again forced to defend itself against the charge that it always seems to be having the undernourished studied by the over-paid. I understand all that. But what does it have to do with what Marc Antony said at Caesar's funeral?

I'll admit that I'm a bit rusty on the subject of ora-tions. I'm not sure I've heard many since the annual public speaking contests I used to attend when I was a student at Southwest High School in Kansas City. Even then, I had trouble telling orations from declama-tions, despite a classmate's having offered me what he claimed to be a sure-fire working definition: "An ora-tion is just a little bit louder." Mistakes in orations were made at the Southwest public speaking contest, of course, but none of them had anything to do with Puerto Ricans. As far as I can remember, the only offense to any minority group came when Leroy Win-net, having got badly stuck during what I thought had been a splendid rendition of Demosthenes' "On the Crown," finally blurted out, "The Greeks was all fairies anyway," and stomped off the stage.

Of course, J. Peter Grace went to St. Paul's School, an *echt*-preppy boarding school, and for all I know the oratorical tradition might have been a bit different there than it was at Southwest. I suppose it's possible that at St. Paul's School oratorical mistakes involving

Puerto Ricans were as common as Topsiders. I can imagine what the annual public speaking contest at St. Paul's might have been like when J. Peter Grace was there. On the stage is Thatcher Baxter Hatcher, the previous year's winner of the Hatcher Prize for Oratory as well as the Thatcher Prize for Being Condescending in Latin or Greek. He is standing nervously at the podium, about to deliver the oration in which Demosthenes denounced the ambitions of Philip of Macedon. "There is a foolish saying of persons who wish to make us easy that Philip is not yet as powerful as the Lacedaemonians were formerly, who ruled everywhere by land and sea, and had the king for their ally, and nothing withstood them," he says. "Yet Athens resisted even that nation, and was not destroyed, not even by an influx of Puerto Ricans."

The judges, stern but kindly old St. Paul's masters, grimace slightly, saddened that such a promising young man as Thatcher Baxter Hatcher has been tripped up by a Puerto Rican mistake. No one knows why the Puerto Rican mistake is so prevalent at St. Paul's School; according to a student legend, it comes from something they put in the mashed potatoes. Then Hatcher's rival — his cousin, Hatcher Thatcher Baxter — steps to the podium. He is presenting Cicero's oration on the conspiracy of Catiline. "What?" Baxter says, sweeping his arm dramatically. "Did not that most illustrious man, Publius Scipio, the Pontifex Maximus, in his capacity of a private citizen, put to death Tiberius Gracchus, though but slightly under-

mining the Constitution by plea-bargaining with Puerto
Ricans? And shall we, who are the consuls, tolerate
Catiline, openly desirous to destroy the whole world
with fire and slaughter and salsa music on those huge
radios they carry?"

Young Baxter is devastated. One by one, though, the
other contestants fall into the same trap. They deliver
orations by Daniel Webster ("If it be the pleasure of
heaven that my country shall require the poor offering
of my life, the victim shall be ready at the appointed
hour of sacrifice, come when that hour may. But while
I do live, let me have a country, or at least the hope of
a country, and that a free country, free from the welfare mothers who can't speak English") and William
Jennings Bryan ("You shall not crucify mankind upon
a cross of Puerto Ricans!").

Then young Peter Grace steps to the podium. He is
the final boy on the program. It is up to him to avoid
a total oratorical disaster for St. Paul's School, and
there is widespread confidence that he will. He is an
outstanding orator. He has been voted Most Likely
to Succeed — his classmates having determined that
his pleasing personality will land him a job at W. R.
Grace & Co. and that his pluck and determination will
take him all the way to the chairmanship. He has
chosen an oration by Patrick Henry. "If we wish to be
free — if we mean to preserve inviolate those inestim-
able privileges for which we have been so long con-
tending — if we mean not basely to abandon the noble
struggle in which we have been so long engaged, and

which we have pledged ourselves never to abandon until the glorious object of our contest shall be obtained," Grace says, "we must send them all back to Ponce."

There is tremendous disappointment at St. Paul's. J. Peter Grace has let down the side. But Peter picks himself up from that disgrace and goes on to fulfill the expectations of his classmates. Eventually he rises to the chairmanship of W. R. Grace & Co., at a salary of $1,809,882 a year. Still, he remains haunted by the fear of making another oratorical mistake of a Puerto Rican nature. For forty years he avoids mashed potatoes, just in case. He is afraid that someday he will repeat the Puerto Rican mistake. One day he does.

Ouch!

_____

August 21, 1982

NOT LONG AGO, I ran across a man who pulls his own teeth. As my father used to say, you meet all kinds. I suppose you're wondering how the subject came up. I suspect you think it came up during one of those frivolous summertime conversations on the beach, when people try to be clever as a way of diverting attention from their waistlines. Somebody says something like, "The way the book business is going these days, I half expect to turn on a talk show and see some shrink in a turtleneck sweater pushing a best seller called *How to Extract Your Own Appendix by Believing in Yourself.*" Everyone chuckles, but then one person on the edge of the crowd — a rather intense-looking person who is wearing sandals and black socks and has a thermos full of lukewarm mineral water with him — says, "As a matter of fact, I pull my own teeth." That is not the way it happened at all.

Now that you know that, you probably think I simply read about this in the newspaper, because a lot of newspaper stories these days are about the sort of people who go on talk shows in turtlenecks to discuss taking out your own appendix. "Two years ago," you imagine the newspaper story saying, "nobody could have predicted that Dr. Marvin Smolin, a successful and conventional suburban dentist, was destined to become the leader of a movement advocating that people pull their own teeth. Dr. Smolin then had a prosperous practice in Bergen County, New Jersey, and was widely known in the New York television world as the technical consultant to the long-running network series based on a father-and-son dental practice — *The Extractors*. He was active in the American Dental Association, having served for three years running as chairman of the ADA's Special Committee on Tax Shelters. 'I was Joe Establishment, D.D.S., but I really didn't know who I was,' Dr. Smolin said yesterday, while in town to conduct a four-day seminar on auto-extractics. 'Just for a start, I thought I was Joe Establishment, D.D.S., and I was really Marvin Smolin.'" That's not how it happened. Not even close. The subject of auto-extraction came up because I noticed a man who was jumping up and down.

It happened in front of a fruit and vegetable stand in my neighborhood. At first, I didn't pay much attention to the man who was jumping up and down, because I assumed he was just reacting to the price of raspberries. That happens a lot in my neighborhood. I've

seen a man stomping on his own hat over what an avo-
cado costs these days. I once saw someone who looked
perfectly normal — which is not, as it happens, the
way most people in my neighborhood look — lying on
his stomach in a produce store and banging on the
floor with his fists in response to what they had the
nerve to charge for one lousy watermelon.

This jumping up and down had nothing to do with
the price of fruit and vegetables. The man involved
was jumping up and down to demonstrate how he
diverts the blood supply from his mouth so there is
less pain when he pulls his own tooth. That you never
guessed. That is how it happened. He was explaining
the entire process to a friend. I overheard everything.
He takes some pill; I can't remember the name of it,
but from the way he described it I assume it's the sort
of thing that might make you feel like having a go at
your spleen once you had your infected molar out of
the way. Then he jumps up and down, and then —
Whammo! — he pulls his own tooth. Other than that,
he looked like an unremarkable fellow, except that he
was missing a lot of teeth. I got the feeling he might
pull a perfectly healthy one now and then just to keep
in practice.

I don't want to talk about the question of whether a
man who pulls his own teeth is the one true practitioner
of holistic medicine. That's not what this is all about.
I know my friend Harold the Committed would have
you believe that this just goes to show that Brute Capitalism, which treats the health of the people as a com-

modity to be bought and sold, has forced auto-extractic practices on decent working men. Sometimes I get awfully tired of Harold the Committed. He may well be right about Brute Capitalism, but as I sized up this fellow who pulls his own teeth — and I'll admit that sizing up a fellow is not that easy to do if he keeps jumping up and down and trying to simulate the effects of a pill that makes you want to have a go at your own spleen — I figured he might be interested in pulling his own teeth even if he could afford the watermelon at my neighborhood fruit and vegetable store.

I suppose by now you must think that what this is all about is some gripe I've been harboring against professional dentistry. Not exactly. As it happens, I did recently have a tooth pulled by a second party. My only complaint was that he threw the tooth away while I was still under the anesthetic — an anesthetic that did not, by the way, summon up in me any enthusiasm for going after my own spleen. I had plans for that tooth. What I had intended to do was to donate it to the American Dental Association and take a write-off of $20,000, which is what I estimated I had put into the tooth over the years. That happens to be a conservative estimate, because I didn't perfect the scheme until I was sitting in the second party's recovery room, still woozy from the anesthetic, and I might have let a root canal or two slip my mind.

I don't blame the dentist who pulled my tooth for not anticipating the use I might have had for an extracted bicuspid — which, not to quibble or make a

big point of it, happened to be my property by the ancient Common Law rules of attachment. I think I'd
let him pull the next one; I'd simply have my account-
ant there to receive it. I don't want to pull my own
teeth. I am still amazed, though, at how plausible it
all sounded at the fruit stand. I remember thinking
that pulling an upper tooth down would be a lot easier
than pulling a lower tooth up. I could almost see myself pulling an upper tooth. I take the pill. I jump up
and down. Then, whammo!

The Novelist Revealed

September 18, 1982

I HAVE TO ADMIT that I didn't know the next thing would be novelists posing nude to the waist in national magazines. I try to keep up, but it's getting harder and harder to know what the next thing is going to be. Even after Jerzy Kosinski was on the cover of the *New York Times Magazine* in half of a polo-playing costume, I didn't know for certain that it was the beginning of the next thing. Sure, I heard some talk about the picture — "Yech!" was one comment I heard — but nobody said, "I guess this is going to be the next thing." Then, on the inside back cover of *The New Yorker*, I saw an ad for *Vanity Fair* which consisted of a color picture of John Irving in most of his old college wrestler's uniform. "I guess this is going to be the next thing," I said to my wife.

"Think of poor Norman Mailer," she said. "Nobody has asked him to pose in his boxing trunks."

"It's only a matter of time," I said. "They'll all get their chance now. Updike will be shown wearing only plaid golf pants and holding a putter. Malamud and Mark Harris will be pictured at adjoining lockers, each of them wearing the bottom half of a Boston Red Sox uniform. Roth will be in his undies. Thomas McGuane will be in hunting pants only, carrying a shotgun. Capote will be in a backgammon club — the only player in the room not wearing a shirt."

"How can you be sure this is going to be the next thing?" my wife said. "Remember the time you thought movie stars were going to start wearing bowling shirts?"

Well, this had the feel of the next thing about it. The next thing is always unexpected — a twist that makes people who didn't know it was coming start sentences with "Who would have thought . . ." Who would have thought, for instance, that novelists would start going around posing for magazines without their shirts on? It's certainly not the sort of thing novelists have made a habit of in the past. Oh, I suppose Hemingway might have had his picture in *Life* once or twice sitting shirtless on a deep-sea fishing boat, but can anyone imagine that there was ever a time when somebody tried to persuade Henry James that, all in all, it might be beneficial to his career if he posed in one of those baggy Victorian bathing costumes for the cover of the *Illustrated London News*? As Mr. James often said, not hardly.

Yes, it's true that in my eagerness to keep up I might have jumped the gun a few times in calling something the next thing. It isn't easy, after all, to think of something nobody would have thought. Once, I was wrong in circumstances very much like those we find ourselves in today. Fifteen years ago, *Harper's Bazaar* ran a picture of a countess nude to the waist. Her name was something like the Countess of Provolone. "This is going to be the next thing," I said right away. "All the countesses are going to have their pictures in fashion magazines nude to the waist. Maybe baronesses too. You heard it here first."

Well, of course that didn't happen. Sure, there have been pictures of a nude countess now and then, but on the whole I would have to say that over the past fifteen or twenty years countesses as an occupational group have done a pretty good job of keeping their clothes on in public. Naturally, the failure of other countesses to follow the Countess of Provolone's example caused me some embarrassment — although not, I suspect, as much as it caused the Countess of Provolone ("Isn't it simply too much, my dear?" I could hear those catty, fully-clothed countesses saying to one another. "Imagine silly Provolone thinking it would be cute to show off her maracas in *Harper's Bazaar!*").

That's why I wouldn't have been ready to say that novelists posing with their shirts off was the next thing just on the evidence of one picture of Jerzy Kosinski on the cover of the *New York Times Magazine*: it reminded me too much of that unfortunate business with the Countess of Provolone. I could just see myself saying, "This is the next thing," and then having the rest of the novelists keep their shirts on and make snide little jokes to each other about the Polish polo team.

Then I saw the picture of John Irving, and I said, "This is going to be the next thing." The picture, after all, was advertising the imminent rebirth of *Vanity Fair*, a magazine that once had the reputation of knowing what the next thing was going to be; for all I know, they might have a picture in their files of Henry James in one of those baggy Victorian bathing costumes. The only question in my mind was how far it would go. I could picture Isaac Bashevis Singer being called in by the trendy young conglomerateur who had just swallowed up his publishing house:

"Welcome aboard, Isaac," the conglomerateur says. "What's your sport?"

"Well, I do a little Talmudic hair-splitting now and then," Singer says. "Just to keep a hand in."

As I was trying to imagine whether the conglomerateur would dare ask Singer if Talmudists, on exceedingly muggy days, ever went about their business wearing just trousers and a prayer shawl, I heard the real voice of Alice. "You don't think *The Nation* will run a full-page ad of Victor S. Navasky in the trunks of his Elisabeth Irwin High School basketball uniform, do you?" she was saying.

The Nixon Library

_____

October 9, 1982

MY AUNT ROSIE called from Kansas City to ask my advice on how she might go about offering her house as a site for the Nixon Presidential Library. "Who's the big enchilada over there?" she said. "I don't want to talk to any clerks."

I have to admit that the request caught me off guard. Like most Midwesterners who have moved to New York City, I get phone calls now and then from relatives back home who have need of some Big Apple guidance, but the usual question is more on the order of how to get tickets to *Annie*. Also, I was obviously surprised to hear someone propose a two-bedroom bungalow in Kansas City as the site of a presidential library — particularly someone who had previously expressed the opinion that an appropriate site for the Nixon library would be the United States Penitentiary at Leavenworth. Also, I don't happen to know the big

· 6 5 ·

enchilada over there. I don't know how to get tickets to *Annie* either.

As it happens, my Aunt Rosie is getting on in years, and I tried to take that into account as I probed gently to find out what she had on her mind. "Aunt Rosie," I said, "I think you may have finally passed over the line from an eccentric old coot to a certified crazy."

"Don't put on any of your big-city airs with me," Aunt Rosie said. "I knew you when you thought *beurre blanc* was the French ambassador."

I really didn't see what a perfectly understandable youthful misapprehension concerning a difficult subject like French diplomacy had to do with what we were discussing, but I didn't press the point with Aunt Rosie. I certainly didn't want to upset her, partly because the youthful misapprehension concerning the French ambassador happens not to be the only youthful misapprehension she knows about.

Then it occurred to me that I might have unwittingly provoked Aunt Rosie's call myself by mentioning to her a few weeks before how sorry I was that I didn't have Nixon to kick around anymore. I'm not afraid to admit it. I'd love to have Nixon to kick around. Listen, I'd settle for Alexander Haig. Aunt Rosie understands that. She's a shrewd old biddy. She knows I miss those Alexander the Grape tantrums. She knows I miss those Alexander Maximus poses. She knows I wince every time I read about what a sane, unthreatened, nonegotistical, low-key team player good old George Shultz is. She knows my basic view of foreign policy: if it all amounts to backing the wrong people in every part of the world anyway, it might as well be done in an entertaining way. Suddenly I was touched by Aunt Rosie's gesture. "Are you doing this for me?" I asked her. "Are you prepared to sacrifice your own home just so Nixon will be back in public view and I'll have a chance to get in a kick or two?"

"Don't flatter yourself, big shot," Aunt Rosie said. "Why should I make any sacrifices for someone who couldn't even come up with *Annie* tickets for the aunt who more than once changed his diapers in his hour of need?"

Then why? Could Aunt Rosie finally have developed some sympathy for Richard M. Nixon after Duke University turned down the library? It's true that there was something sad about how the towns that expressed interest in having it got more and more obscure — first places like Independence, Missouri, and then places like Baker, Oregon. Did she really think that the only way to stop that embarrassing downward spiral was to offer what had been my cousin Norman's bedroom? That didn't sound like Aunt Rosie. She's a tough old bird. Nixon's constant presentation of himself as a victim, in fact, was what she found most repellent about him. "The man has raised the whine to an art form," she always said. She routinely referred to him as "King of the Kvetches." Although I don't mean to bring up the matter in a self-serving way, it might be relevant to point out that Aunt Rosie didn't exhibit much sympathy when it came to considering the difficulties that might be entailed in getting into a musical that at the time happened to be the hottest ticket on Broadway.

"Just give me the enchilada's name and number," Aunt Rosie said. "I'll take it from there."

"If you're thinking mainly of some way to put Cousin Norman's room to good use, don't you think a boarder would be a better idea?" I said. I tried to explain to Aunt Rosie that the historical artifacts alone in such a library would strain the space available in Norman's room, even on the unlikely chance that she finally got Norman's permission to dispose of his old butterfly collection. I tried to explain to Aunt Rosie that a presidential library would generate the sort of traffic that would simply not be acceptable to someone who has always been particularly concerned about the danger that mud might be tracked in onto her living room carpet. "There's no way to get to Norman's room without going through the living room," I said — making what I figured was my most telling point.

"Don't tell me you actually think there's any possibility of having a presidential library in Norman's bedroom," Aunt Rosie said. "Do you think, maybe, that just because Nixon was a twerp of a President he'll have a twerp-sized presidential library?"

"There's been some misunderstanding here," I said. "Didn't you just ask how to offer your house as a site for the Nixon Presidential Library?"

"Of course I'm offering," Aunt Rosie said. "Do you think Baker, Oregon, is offering because it really expects to be chosen? They just want the publicity to put Baker on the map."

"You mean you want to be on the map?"

"I was thinking more of an appearance on *Real People* or maybe a guest shot on *Hollywood Squares*," Aunt Rosie said. "Then to the talk-show circuit. I'll be famous. I'll have my own press agent. He'll get me theater tickets."

"But I don't know the big enchilada over there," I finally admitted.

"I didn't think you would," Aunt Rosie said. "I always told your mother you'd never amount to anything."

The 401st

October 30, 1982

"YOU MUST get over this," Alice said. "It's misplaced sympathy."

I couldn't get over it. The minute I saw *Forbes* magazine's list of the four hundred richest people in the United States, my heart went out to the person who was four hundred and first.

"He's nothing but some rich creep," Alice said.

"Creeps have feelings too," I said. The phrase she had used suddenly conjured up a picture of the poor soul I was worrying about: Rich Creep, the Manhattan megadeal cutter and man about town. He lives in the Carlyle. He dates models. He eats breakfast at the Regency, where deals are made so quickly that a careless conglomerateur could find himself swallowing up a middle-sized corporation while under the impression that he was just mopping up his egg yolk with the end of a croissant. He dines every night at places like La Caravelle and Le Cirque. "*Bonsoir*, Monsieur Cripp,"

· 70 ·

the headwaiter says when Creep walks in with an icily beautiful fashion model who weighs eighty-eight pounds, twelve of which are in cheekbones. "If I may make a suggestion, the overpriced veal is excellent tonight."

On the way to breakfast one morning, Creep happens to see the cover of *Forbes* at the Carlyle newsstand. "The Richest People in America," the headline says. "The *Forbes* Four Hundred." He snatches the magazine from the rack and, standing right in the lobby, he starts going through the list — at first methodically and then desperately. Finally, he turns and slinks back to his room. He can't face the crowd at the Regency. They'd pretend nothing has changed, but then they'd start trying to find some smaller corporation for him to swallow up — the way a nanny might sort through the picnic basket to find the smallest piece of white meat for the least adventurous child. He cancels his dinner date for the evening. He's afraid he might be given a cramped table near the kitchen, where the draft from the swinging doors could blow the fashion model into the dessert cart. He's afraid that the same French waiters who once hovered over him attentively while he ate ("Is your squab done expensively enough, Monsieur Cripp?") will glance in his direction and whisper to each other, *"Les petites pommes de terre"* — small potatoes.

"People are beginning to talk about how often you express sympathy for rich people," Alice said.

That may be true. When everyone else was looking

among the impoverished for what Reagan meant by "truly needy," I called attention to the plight of Philip Caldwell, the chairman of the Ford Motor Company, who was denied an incentive bonus two years in a row even though I have every reason to believe that he was going flat-out the whole time. When the Reagan nominee for chairman of the synfuels corporation, a lawyer from Greenwich, Connecticut, said that the proposed salary of $150,000 was so far below a living wage that he might be forced to move out of Greenwich, I tried to bring to the world's attention what a sad spectacle it would be if everyone who made less than $150,000 a year had to leave Greenwich, moving west in a caravan of station wagons like a preppy *Grapes of Wrath.*

"I suppose you're going to say, 'The rich are different from you and me,'" Alice said.

She was referring, of course, to that famous exchange between two great American literary figures — when Zane Grey said to Will Rogers, "The rich are different from you and me," and Rogers replied, "Yes, they don't wear cowboy boots." Was it when rich people began wearing cowboy boots that I included them in my concerns? No, it was long before that. It was when *Fortune* first published its list of the five hundred largest corporations in America. My heart went out immediately to the corporation that was five hundred and first.

Of course, I had no way of knowing its name — that tragic anonymity was the basis for my sym-

pathy — but I always thought of it as Humboldt Bolt
& Tube. I felt for the folks at Humboldt Bolt & Tube.
I could see them giving their all to build their corporation into one of the largest corporations in America —
busting unions, cutting corners on safety specifica-
tions, bribing foreign heads of state, slithering out
of expensive pollution-control regulations — only to
remain unrecognized year after year.

As the Fortune 500 became an institution in American life, I often pictured the scene at the Humboldt
Country Club in Humboldt, Ohio, when an important
visitor from Wall Street asks casually over drinks, "Do
you have any Fortune 500 companies in Humboldt?"

For a moment, no one speaks. The "old man," as
everyone in Humboldt calls Harrison H. Humboldt,
the son of Bolt & Tube's founder, looks out at the
eighteenth green, the hint of a tear in his eye. Finally,
someone says, "No, but we've got the third largest
granite pit east of the Mississippi."

"You simply can't take this on while you still insist
on worrying about that silly bolt company," Alice said.

It's true that my feelings about the folks at Humboldt remain intense — particularly just after the Fortune 500 list comes out each year. I can see old
Harrison H. Humboldt sitting in his office, looking
disconsolate. Just missed again. Has it all been worth
it? His son is a cipher who keeps talking about "in-
put." The line workers whose fathers used to call him
H.H. are a bunch of Bolshevik hippies. His grandson
answered the most recent inquiry about what he in-

tended to make of his life by saying, "I'm into cocaine, Gramps, and the rock zither." A trusted aide says, "Cheer up, H.H. You're one of the richest men in the country."

But is he? I grabbed *Forbes* from the coffee table, and raced through the list. Harrison H. Humboldt's name was not there. Parvenu oilmen were there. New York real estate sharks were there. Coca-Cola bottlers were there. But not Harrison H. Humboldt. Just missed again.

"You have to forget about this creep," Alice said.

"You're right," I said. "I don't think Creep even deserves to be listed. Compared to a man like Harrison H. Humboldt, he's small potatoes."

Harold the Committed

November 20, 1982

A COUPLE OF WEEKS ago, my acquaintance Harold the Committed asked me if I wanted to see civilization as we know it destroyed in a nuclear holocaust, and I had to admit that I didn't. It happens that he had asked the same question a few weeks before, and I had given him the same answer. I can't imagine what led him to think that my position on the destruction-of-civilization issue might have wavered in such a short time. What kind of person does Harold the Committed think I am? Sure, there are days when things don't go quite the way I had hoped they would. Occasionally I go through what I think of as a multimotor day: the automobile repairman says we need a new motor, the dishwasher repairman says we need a new motor, the clothes-dryer repairman says we need a new motor. Even on a multimotor day, though, I don't sit down with a drink when it's all over and say to myself, "Well, if that's the way it's going to be, I would like to see civilization as we know it destroyed in a nuclear holocaust." I'm much more likely to say something like, "But didn't we just *get* a new motor for the dishwasher?"

I didn't go into all of that with Harold the Committed, of course. That's the sort of thing that can hurt Harold's feelings, and he's got enough trouble as it is — what with the refugee problem in Africa and repression in South America and the steady loss of topsoil in the Midwest. What I said to Harold the Committed in answer to his question was, "I've given this issue a lot of thought, Hal the C, and I remain firmly opposed to the destruction of civilization as we know it in a nuclear holocaust. You can count on me on this one."

"What are you doing about it?" Harold the Committed said.

"As it happens, you've caught me at a bad time, Harold the Committed," I said. "You know I'm not very political just before Halloween."

I wasn't just spinning an alibi for Harold the Committed. Just before Halloween, I always have a lot on my mind. For one thing, I have to decide on a costume for the Halloween parade. Are people getting tired of my ax murderer's mask? Should I take advantage of my uncanny ability to bark like a dog by going as an unhappy Airedale? Harold the Committed finds it difficult to understand how I can spend so much time agonizing over a costume for the Halloween parade; he goes every year as an unemployed coal miner.

My Halloween responsibilities go well beyond my own costume. I have to be a consultant to my daughters in the matter of their costumes, since my wife's attitude toward Halloween, I regret to say, borders on the blasé. I have to take part in serious discussions about the possibility that my daughters and I might encourage my wife to wear something more appropriate than a token witch hat.

"Daddy, I don't really think you're going to be able to persuade Mommy to wear that long, crooked witch's nose with the warts on it," one of them is likely to say.

"Well, how about these individual, rubberized, easy-to-remove face warts?" I say hopefully.

Although the old political saw holds that the electorate doesn't pay complete attention to a national political campaign until after the World Series, I find that my attention is not really engaged until after Halloween. Some years, of course, that gives me only two or three days to concentrate on the campaign, but I usually find that sufficient: if I have trouble making up my mind, I simply ask Harold the Committed which candidate is less likely to follow policies that might lead to the destruction of civilization as we know it in a nuclear holocaust. This year, the two days of campaign commercials I took in made me grateful I hadn't paid much attention before, since a lot of them seemed to feature members of the candidate's family talking about why he should be elected. I could envision one of my daughters looking straight into the camera and saying, "Please send my daddy to Congress because then he won't be around as much to embarrass us in public by barking like a dog."

"Halloween can be approached as an opportunity," Harold the Committed said. "Like any other public event, it can be used as a platform for making a political statement."

The last time Harold the Committed started talking about Halloween that way he ended by suggesting that my ten-year-old daughter, Sarah, go to the Halloween parade costumed as Emma Goldman. She decided to go as a chocolate-chocolate-chip ice cream cone with chocolate sprinkles instead.

"What's your daughter Sarah going as this year?" Harold the Committed asked.

"She's leaning toward the idea of going as a jar of Hellmann's mayonnaise, Hal the C," I said.

"She really doesn't have a lot of political awareness, does she?" Harold the Committed said.

"It's not her awareness she's worried about, it's other people's," I said. "Last year not everybody was aware that she was supposed to be a chocolate-chocolate-chip ice cream cone with chocolate sprinkles. A couple of people thought she was a tube of toothpaste. She figures a mayonnaise jar would be a little more explicit."

I knew what was coming next, and, sure enough, Harold repeated a suggestion he seems to make every year: "Maybe your daughter Abigail could go as the dangers posed to our society by the military-industrial complex."

"We don't have anybody at home who can sew that well, Hal the C," I said. "Abigail's going as an M & M." Abigail has never been much impressed with Harold's costume suggestions, particularly since he persuaded his niece to go as a peace dove and everyone thought she was supposed to be Donald Duck.

"It's a matter of paying lip service or making a political statement through every aspect of your life," Harold the Committed said. "Everyone must make a decision."

"I've decided, Hal the C," I said. "I'm going as an ax murderer again after all."

Confessions of a Dupe

―――

"YOU LOOK MAD. Did something bad happen at school?"

"Daddy, this rotten kid in my class said that you're a dupe of the Communists. I told him you're *not* a dupe — you just do dupey things sometimes, like barking like a dog in public."

"Not dupey — dopey."

"Why did he say you're a dupe?"

"It has to do with a literary dispute."

"I didn't know you were literary. If you're literary, why does Mommy have to explain foreign movies to you?"

"It's too complicated for a little girl to understand."

"That's what you always say if I ask you about a movie before Mommy has explained it to you."

"All right. I'll try to explain. A writer named Jerzy Kosinski came here from Poland, and within a few years he was spending a lot of time at fancy dinner

Confessions of a Dupe

parties with movie stars and dress designers and countesses from New Jersey and the editors of the *New York Times* — and that was good because it was a refutation of the vile ethnic slur that Poles don't catch on quickly. Apparently, one of the reasons he was so popular at dinner parties was that he told very entertaining little fibs about growing up in Poland."

"You mean the way you tell little fibs about growing up in Kansas City? Like how the American Hereford Association building has a bull on top of it whose heart and liver light up at night?"

"Well, on the Hereford bull issue, I'd just like to say —"

"Maybe we could talk about the Hereford bull later."

"O.K. Well, the dress designers just smiled at the little fibs, because they hear little fibs on Seventh Avenue all the time — about how soon the garments will be delivered and when the check was put in the mail and that sort of thing. Unfortunately for Kosinski, though, the editors of the *New York Times* must have taken him seriously."

"I thought newspaper editors were supposed to be skeptical, Daddy."

"Only of people who are not invited to the same dinner parties. Barbara Gelb, whose husband is one of the most important *Times* editors at any dinner table, wrote an article on Kosinski for the *Times* magazine that was so gushy that some people — myself included, I'm afraid — commented on how fortunate she had been that he had restrained himself from telling her that he was, in point of fact, the long-lost Princess Anastasia."

"Anastasia of Russia? Is that where the Communists come in?"

"No, no. What happened was that the *Village Voice* ran an article showing that some of the stories Barbara Gelb had swallowed — like Kosinski's story about how he got out of Poland — were what literary people call Easter Bunny stuff. The real point of the *Village Voice* article, though, was to claim that Kosinski got a little help with his novels, the way I sometimes give you a little help with your homework."

"I hope he at least found people who understand math."

"Well, it turned out that nobody but the *Village Voice* seemed much interested in whether Kosinski got a little help with his novels or not. In a few months, everyone had forgotten all about it — except, unfortunately for Kosinski, the editors of the *New York Times*, who must have been very embarrassed about the Easter Bunny stuff. They got someone to do a very long article on Kosinski's enemies that read like the sort of article Jack Valenti might have written in 1967 on the enemies of Lyndon B. Johnson. It said that all of the suspicion about Kosinski's not writing his own books had been planted by a wicked Polish Communist. Then William Safire wrote a column in the *Times* saying that the left-wing literati were picking on Kosinski just because he had criticized *The Nation*'s Writers

Congress and didn't conform to 'prevailing leftist maunderings.' "

"What does 'maunderings' mean?"

"I'm not quite sure."

"How can you be one of the literati if you don't even know what 'maunderings' means?"

"So far, that's my best defense."

"And, Daddy, Mommy said you fell asleep at *The Nation*'s Writers Congress."

"There's another defense right there."

"Well, how did Kosinski really get out of Poland?"

"My theory is that Oscar and Françoise de la Renta phoned him in Warsaw and asked him to dinner. The regime gave him what they call a 'dinner-party visa,' because they figured that if they allowed Kosinski to go to the de la Rentas he would get in with a fancy crowd. Then if the Polish economy was about to collapse and Solidarity threatened and the Russian Army was at the border, they could at least launch an international Communist plot to smear the Gelbs as social climbers."

"Listen, Daddy, you're not talking to the *New York Times* now, so don't try any of that Easter Bunny stuff. Did you ever meet this wicked Polish Communist?"

"A man sleeping next to me at the Writers Congress had a sort of foreign look, but he may have just been a hippie."

"Then who do you think has been spreading the rumors that Kosinski didn't write his own books?"

"I just this moment realized: it may have been Kosinski."

"Kosinski!"

"Of course Kosinski. Have you read the reviews of his last few books?"

"You're talking to a little girl, Daddy. I don't keep up with reviews. Now, if I had someone who understood math helping me with my homework, I might have time —"

"Never mind. I'll tell you: the black plague got a more respectful reception. Why didn't I see it before? This way, Kosinski gets paid for the books and someone else gets blamed for writing them."

"Just wait till I get to school tomorrow. I'm going to tell that rotten kid a thing or two."

"What are you going to tell him?"

"I'm going to tell him you're a dupe of Jerzy Kosinski."

My Tuxedo

January 1, 1983

I AM OFTEN MISTAKEN for the sort of person who does not own a tuxedo. Once or twice, I regret to say, this mistake has been made even though I happened to be wearing a tuxedo at the time ("My goodness, are they still renting that kind?"). More often, it is part of a general impression. "I don't suppose you own a tuxedo . . ." people sometimes say to me, the way an English country gentleman might say to the Hasidic scholar he has met on the train, "I don't suppose you own a shooting stick . . ." The general impression is incorrect. I do own a tuxedo. I have owned a tuxedo for nearly thirty years. The same tuxedo. If you were planning to invite me to an event at which tuxedos are required, rest assured that I would show up properly dressed.

Don't ask me for New Year's Eve. I'm busy. I go to the same party every New Year's Eve, and one reason it gives me great pleasure is that it presents me with an opportunity to wear my tuxedo. I bought the tuxedo in 1954, when I was a thrifty young undergraduate, because I had added up the number of black-tie events I would have to attend during college, divided the cost of a tuxedo by that number, and concluded that I would be better off buying a tuxedo than renting one. As you must have gathered, this was a fancy college. I am often mistaken for the sort of person who did not attend a fancy college, but that's another story.

As it turned out, there have been a number of occasions to wear the tuxedo since graduation — that possibility hadn't even figured in my tuxedo management scheme in 1954 — and every time I wear it the cost per wearing decreases. This New Year's Eve, for instance, wearing my tuxedo is going to cost me only about forty-eight cents. Try renting a tuxedo for forty-eight cents these days. Knowing that my tuxedo becomes cheaper every time I wear it may influence me in the direction of showing up in a tuxedo now and then at events where black-tie is not strictly necessary, like a hog roast or a divorce hearing or a meeting where people are planning the overthrow of the government by force and violence.

"Oh, you shouldn't have bothered," the hostess often says, while gazing admiringly at my cummerbund.

"It's nothing, really," I tell her. "A matter of approximately fifty-five cents."

When I tell people about my tuxedo ("Guess how much this tuxedo is costing me tonight. Go ahead — don't be afraid to guess. Just take a guess. How much do you think?"), they often tell me that I should be proud of being able to fit into something I bought in college. True. I would be prouder, though, if I did not have reason to believe that the pants of my tuxedo actually belong to Joe LeBeau. Joe was a college classmate of mine — a rather rotund college classmate of mine, if you must know. I have reason to believe that just before graduation, at a black-tie party for which a large room was converted into a dormitory for a number of out-of-town guests who were wearing nearly identical tuxedos, Joe LeBeau and I came away with each other's pants. That's the sort of thing that can happen at a fancy college.

When somebody who sees me in my tuxedo asks a question that leads to the subject of Joe LeBeau ("Say, are you by any chance wearing somebody else's pants, or what?"), I am often asked why I did not simply exchange his pants for my own once the mistake was discovered. Anybody who asks that never knew Joe LeBeau, for whom the phrase "not vulnerable to reason" was invented. As an example of LeBeauesque conversation, I repeat an exchange between LeBeau and an earnest fellow from down the hall who happened to be taking the same course in modern history:

JOE LEBEAU: The French and Germans were fighting on the same side then.
EARNEST FELLOW: But that's impossible! The French hated the Germans!
JOE LEBEAU: Do you blame them?

I haven't seen Joe LeBeau since graduation — I understand he's a judge in California — but I occasionally run into other classmates who, as graduates of a fancy college, tend to be Wall Street financiers, impatient with those of us who have not just depreciated a factory or written off an airline. "What are you up to?" they always say.

"I am amortizing my tuxedo," I tell them. "I am amortizing the hell out of my tuxedo."

By exchanging such pleasantries with the rich, I realize, I continue to disappoint Harold the Committed, who continues to worry a lot about the possibility that I am not worrying enough.

"What are you doing about the finite supply of natural resources on this planet?" he said only the other day.

"I'm glad you asked, Hal the C," I replied. "As it happens, I have been wearing the same tuxedo now for nearly thirty years. No squandering of the earth's irreplaceable fossil fuels to produce a new tuxedo every season for me. Nobody's clear-cutting any forests to make me a tuxedo. Little children in Europe aren't starving while I leave perfectly good tuxedos on my plate."

Harold the Committed, after reminding me that the Scottsboro Boys didn't own even one tuxedo among them, said that I was badly in need of attending one of his regular recommitment meetings.

"Any time but New Year's Eve," I said. "I'm busy on New Year's Eve."

My Tuxedo

I can see my New Year's Eve now. I am dressing for the evening. I calculate what my tuxedo is going to cost me to wear to the same party one year hence, assuming I wear it occasionally during the intervening months — to a turkey shoot, say, or a bris. Even taking the voluminous pants off the hanger gives me pleasure. I find it a bit awkward putting on Joe LeBeau's pants, of course, but I love to start the new year by thinking of him trying to put on mine.

Too Soon to Tell

January 29, 1983

I HAD ASSUMED that during this month — the traditional time for midterm toting up, national stocktaking, and Washington thumb-sucking — people would be asking me a lot of questions about Deity Overload. These kinds of questions: Has the period of the most acute danger of Deity Overload passed? Has the economy become a factor? How do you see Deity Overload affecting the Western alliance? Will Deity Overload be a major factor in the second half of Ronald Reagan's term? Will Ronald Reagan be a major factor in the second half of Ronald Reagan's term?

I was ready for them. "To pose the question in terms of 'liberal' or 'conservative' is to misunderstand it" was one of the answers I had worked up. "It's too soon to tell" was another. "It's too soon to tell" is one of my favorite answers for any question; it's that rare phrase that permits you to sound more informed by saying you don't know. Just the other day, one of my daughters said, "How do you find the area of an isosceles triangle, Daddy?" and I said, "It's too soon to tell." If cornered on the Deity Overload issue, I was prepared to go all the way: I was prepared to say, "One simply doesn't know."

Nobody has asked me about Deity Overload. Maybe they think Deity Overload will obviously have no effect on the Western alliance or that the period of the most acute danger passed months ago. Or maybe they're asking someone else. Maybe they forgot that I was the one who first called attention to the danger of Deity Overload. The public memory is short, after all. Just the other night, as I was eating a plate of picadillo with black beans and rice on the side, it occurred to me that everyone has forgotten about the Russian combat brigade in Cuba, only sixty miles off our shore. Nobody has even mentioned those Russians in years. For all we know, they might have reached Miami by now. As it happens, Miami these days is the sort of place where a Russian combat brigade could show up without attracting much attention. If they're still in Cuba, aren't they getting homesick? Do they try to get a little taste of Mother Russia by having half of the brigade stand in long lines for the wrong size shoes while the other half throws snow on them? Where do they get the snow? It's too soon to tell.

It might be advisable to remind everyone precisely how the danger of Deity Overload first came to public attention. I did it, all by myself. This was at the beginning of the Reagan Administration, when there were a lot of stories going around about how James Watt, a committed Christian who had been appointed Secretary of Drilling, considered no matter too small to benefit from a prayerful request for divine guidance. This, if you'll try to remember, was just after the Reverend Jerry Falwell had asked God to help the Moral Majority defeat a bunch of Congressmen who were blasphemers, drunkards, idolaters, and, on their better days, fornicators. It occurred to me that God already had, as the British ambassador might put it, a lot on His plate.

Was I denying the omnipotence of the Divine Being? To state the question in those terms is to misunderstand it. I was not saying that God has any limits on His powers, only on His patience. I fully understood that Watt might need divine guidance on the big issues. If there came a time, for instance, when he had to decide whether to turn Zion National Park over to Exxon or to preserve it for Mobil, it seemed reasonable for him to ask for a little help. What worried me was the thought that Watt might be asking for divine intervention when he wasn't sure how much of a raise to give his driver or was trying to decide whether wearing a cowboy hat on a trip to Montana might persuade people that he was not, in fact, a wonk.

Here is God, as I envision it, dealing with the usual — five or six wars, a flood here, pestilence there, a billion or two serious commandment-breakers. He's got Jehovah's Witnesses and Seventh-Day Adventists jabbering away at Him day and night. Falwell is pressing for a day-of-rest easement to give Congressmen PAC money on the Sabbath. In the midst of all this, here comes James Watt to ask about cowboy hats. Would it be surprising if, at that point, God said, "Enough's enough"? That would be Deity Overload.

So has the most acute danger of Deity Overload passed, now that the parks are safely in the hands of the oil companies and Jerry Falwell seems to have joined the Russian combat brigade in Cuba? No. The economy has become a factor. A lot of people now have the need for divine intervention in matters that rank in importance somewhere between war and cowboy hats. Given the state of the economy, I can imagine plenty of people saying something like, "If you can't save my store, God, could you at least give the discounter across the street psoriasis?"

And the implications of the international situation? Good question. The implications are enormous. Every morning Ayatollah Khomeini comes in to present God with the news that fifteen or twenty people were executed the previous night for His greater glory — giving God the names of a banker here and a university professor there, the way an overeager cocker spaniel might drop dead sparrows at the feet of its master. Then Menachem Begin appears to remind God about His promise of all Judea and Samaria. "Yes, I know there were a lot of gods in those days," Begin says, "but you were definitely the one we talked to." He is waved away, but reappears almost immediately, saying, "Remember — *all* Judea and Samaria. All of

Judea. Also all of Samaria. Did I mention milk and honey?" There are fourteen wars going on. From Cuba, several hundred Russian soldiers and Jerry Falwell are trying to make a deal with God to trade their immortal souls for not having to listen to one more four-hour speech by Fidel Castro. Khomeini shows up again with the corpses of four newspaper editors and a labor leader. Begin is holding a map that shows Samaria to have extended to the suburbs of Istanbul. Watt is asking whether the cowboy hat may not simply make him look like rough trade. Has the point of Deity Overload been reached? One simply doesn't know.

morning paper. "He's at that age," the United Parcel Service deliveryman explained to my wife. "His hormones are starting to act up on him." Wrong. My hormones are just fine, thank you. Look to your own hormones, United Parcel Service deliveryman. "He's depressed because he sees himself slipping," another lay analyst said, after observing me while he was in the house to unstop a clogged drain. "I've seen it on a lot of jobs lately. He knows he's starting to throw a step behind the runner."

Wrong again. That is not why I quit reading the morning paper. I quit because I was starting to come across the names of people I knew, and it was scaring the hell out of me. Sure, I had borne up under it stoically for a while. I didn't say anything when I read that the trustee chosen to preside over some important estate was a childhood neighbor of mine who had regularly cheated his little sister at old maid. People change. Maybe selling answers to the ninth-grade algebra test — answers, I happen to know, that were worked out by the weird but brilliant Norton Gonsheimer on a promise (never kept) of 40 percent of the action — does not indicate a deep, immutable streak of dishonesty. Who was I to interfere? I remained calm when I read that the new chief of surgery at a fancy hospital uptown was someone who, I happen to know, was held back in the third grade for klutziness. I certainly didn't say anything when I read that one sector of the U.S. Army's missile-alert force was under the command of someone I knew in college as

Dipso Dick Donnigan. What the Russians don't know, I figured, won't hurt them.

When I read that Dalt Durfee had been sent over to work out our trade difficulties with the Japanese, I said a little something. I said, "Dalt Durfee! That pea-brain! Jesus Christ Almighty!" Or words to that effect. I might have said more, I'll admit, if my wife hadn't shot me an odd look and told me I was frightening the children. The reason that the news about Dalt Durfee pushed me over the edge was that I finally realized what was happening. When people around the country read in the morning paper that L. Dalton Durfee, Deputy Undersecretary of State for Asian Economic Affairs, was going to sort things out with the Japanese, they felt reassured that somebody as important as a deputy undersecretary was looking into the matter, and they continued breakfast secure in the expectation that they'd soon be able to buy something that was actually made in America besides hairspray and trash bags. I realized, though, that the person walking around in the role of Deputy Undersecretary of State was, in fact, Dalt Durfee, the fourth dumbest guy in my college class — someone whose most penetrating display of intellectual curiosity had been when he asked a professor of geology whether A.M. means morning or afternoon. I realized that the Japanese would have California before the year was out. Worse than that, I finally realized that every deputy under-secretary was known way-back-when by someone like me. At that point I gave up reading the morning paper.

Why, then, did the symptoms persist? Why did I continue in a funk that inspired the postman to explain to my wife that many men grow listless at a certain age because their thoughts start to dwell morbidly on the future of their prostates. The symptoms persisted because I realized that the people I knew back-when were not simply in the newspaper; they were in the Yellow Pages. When I was staring out the window and the postman thought I was thinking of prostates, I was actually thinking of all the people listed in the Yellow Pages under Attorneys. I know some of those people. It scares me.

In Toledo, the listing includes Ralph W. Moshler, Esq. It's really Blinko Moshler, the dumbest guy in my class — a man who could stand in the intellectual shadow cast by Dalt Durfee and never see the sun. When Durfee asked the professor of geology whether A.M. meant morning or afternoon, Blinko, who was pushy as well as dumb, waved his hand and shouted, "Afternoon! It means afternoon!" How, you ask, did someone as dumb as Blinko Moshler get through law school? If law school is hard to get through, I answer, how come there are so many lawyers?

Blinko is with a respectable firm. People who don't know any better think he's a lawyer named Ralph W. Moshler, Esq. I worry about that. Sometimes, when I'm waiting to fall asleep at night, I worry about a decent, hard-working young man from a very small town in Ohio who goes to Toledo to get factory work. He lives quietly in a boarding house. He's saving his money so he can go back to his little town and open a Burger King franchise. One day, his landlady is brutally murdered. Circumstantial evidence points to the young boarder, although he is, of course, completely innocent. He has no money for a lawyer. The judge says, "I have appointed an attorney to represent you — a prominent member of the bar named Ralph W. Moshler."

"Stop!" I shout. "It's not a lawyer! It's Blinko! He's a mushhead! It's Blinko!"

My wife shakes me awake. "You were talking in your sleep again," she says. "You must be getting to that age."

Invitations

MY CURIOSITY about the new *Vanity Fair* has been dominated by one question: Why wasn't I asked to subscribe? Plenty of people were. I happen to know that one J. E. Corr, Jr., who describes himself as the publisher of *Vanity Fair*, sent letters to any number of people informing them by name ("Dear Mr. Upscale") that his magazine wasn't meant for everyone but for "only a handful of bright, literate people." I'm not saying I look forward to a scene a year or so from now in which some high-powered ad-agency man asks J. E. Corr, Jr., about his circulation and Corr, Jr., says, "Oh, well, about a handful." That would be sour grapes. I will say that it's not a lot of fun being among those for whom a new magazine "that captures the sparkle and excitement of our times, our culture" was not meant.

This has happened to me before. A few years ago, a friend of mine phoned and asked, "What are you doing about Robert L. Schwartz's letter on subscribing to the *Newsletter of the Tarrytown Group?*"

"What letter?" I said.

"You know," he said. "The one that says, 'You are cordially invited to join a special, special group of people — the "Creative Minority," as Toynbee called it — who are stimulated, not threatened, by the changes, upheavals, and discontinuities of modern society. It's a group of people who won't settle for the hollow victory of material success — an idealistic, holistic group that seeks totally new perspectives and concepts to bring about a totally new world for everyone.'"

"Well," I said. "Of course the way the mails are these days, you can't —"

"Oh," he said. "Oh, sorry."

"Maybe Schwartz knew how I feel about people who refer to anything but holes as holistic," I said. I shouldn't have said that. It sounded like sour grapes. Also, I don't mean to give the impression that I can't rejoice with my friends when they are among the chosen. I was delighted, for instance, when a woman I know named Millicent Osborn — a woman who lives in one of those rather grand old Park Avenue apartment buildings that must strike people like J. E. Corr, Jr., as the sort of place where the elevator chatter is particularly bright and literate — received an exceedingly complimentary letter from John Fairchild, whose company publishes *Women's Wear Daily* and *W*. Fairchild thought Mrs. Osborn might like to subscribe to

W. "Our compliments, Mrs. Osborn!" he wrote. "For being one of the best-dressed people in New York! For turning 954 Park Avenue into a home that sizzles with decorating excitement! For giving parties that are the talk of the whole state of New York! For getting the fun out of the fashionable living you do!" Fairchild laying it on makes J. E. Corr, Jr., sound practically curt.

I have always liked to think that Fairchild's letter made Millicent Osborn's day. I realize that there are residents of 954 Park Avenue who would not be particularly gratified to hear that their parties are being talked about in places like Buffalo and Elmira, but Millicent Osborn has never suffered from that sort of insularity. I like to think that she picked up Fairchild's letter in the lobby as she was leaving for the supermarket — at a time in her daily routine when she was not feeling her absolutely most stupefyingly glamorous. She opens the letter. John Fairchild is calling her one of the best-dressed people in New York.

"Oh, it's just a simple little shift I've had for years," she says, causing the doorman to tip his hat. "Do you really like it?"

Then she scurries around to make sure that 954 Park Avenue sizzles with decorating excitement. "The grocery delivery boy told me that the Pearces in 12-D still have that dreadful tapestry of a stag at bay," she tells her husband. "Maybe you could have a word with them."

I also do not want to leave the impression that I have never been selected myself. Just two or three years ago, I got a friendly letter from a Nancy L. Halbert informing me that "the family name Trillin has an exclusive and particularly beautiful Coat of Arms." That was a nice surprise. I don't mean I had been under the impression that our family lacks distinction. For years, I have seized every opportunity to inform the public that my cousin Keith from Salina once reached the finals of the Kansas state spelling bee and my cousin Neil was the drum major of the University of Nebraska marching band. It's not really what you'd call an old family, though, unless Miss Halbert was thinking of my grandfather and my Uncle Benny Daynovsky, who were both then in their nineties.

My grandfather grew up in one of those European towns that used to change countries every week or ten days, and the only claim to distinction I ever heard him make was that he had deserted two separate armies. My Uncle Benny managed to make it from the Ukraine to Missouri early in the century, but I hadn't thought of his passage as the stuff coats of arms are made of. At a family gathering when he was eighty-eight, I happened to remark that I was planning to write something about him in a magazine, and his son said, "Don't mention his name. The Russian army's still looking for him."

I couldn't help but wonder whether these facts were known to the special artist who had, according to Nancy Halbert, already researched and re-created the Trillin Coat of Arms "exactly as the heralds of medieval times did it for the knights and noblemen." I didn't send her $19.95 to find out; I was afraid John Fairchild might not agree with Miss Halbert that a coat of arms adds "warmth and refinement" to any living room, and I was beginning to get the feeling that the decisions I made in these matters were not escaping the notice of Fairchild and other people whose correspondence I valued.

That feeling became intense last spring when Lawrence Gordon, the assistant manager of the Grand Central general office of the New York Life Insurance Company, wrote to say how pleased I would be to know that I had been highly recommended for an opening in his organization. I was pleased in a way — Gordon had so much confidence in me that he even enclosed a card I could send in with the names of people I myself might highly recommend; he apparently had a number of openings — but I had to wonder what qualities he had noticed in me that led him to believe life insurance was my game.

By then, I often imagined a few of the letter writers meeting over martinis and mailing lists to discuss my case. "What about Trillin?" I could imagine J. E. Corr, Jr., of *Vanity Fair* saying.

"Trillin who?" says Robert Schwartz of the *Newsletter of the Tarrytown Group*.

"His family's got an awfully nice coat of arms," Nancy Halbert says. Good old Nancy Halbert. No sour grapes for her just because someone had been forced, through no fault of his own, to stick her with an exclusive coat of arms her special heraldic artists had already researched and re-created. "It's got a lovely border," she continues, "with a bribed immigration officer looking away from it. The center section has crossed steerage tickets rampant on a field of greenhorns."

"Holistically," Schwartz says, "I think he might not interface creatively with your concepts. Also, he's a smart aleck."

"His home doesn't sizzle in the least," John Fairchild says. "I can't imagine who advised him to hang that American Hereford Association poster in the front hall."

"But is he bright and literate?" Corr, Jr., says, consulting his notes. "Does he still make the effort to go to the theater and important films, live concerts, art and photography exhibits?"

"I understand Gordon asked him to join New York Life," Schwartz says.

"Must have been highly recommended," my friend Nancy Halbert says.

"Do you know a lot of bright, literate insurance salesmen?" Schwartz asks.

The room is silent. "I guess we'll give him a skip," Corr, Jr., finally says. "After all, we're only looking for a handful."

Investment Opportunities

March 21, 1983

THOSE WHO THINK that our family is a bit listless about looking after our financial affairs are apparently unaware of the sort of effort we put into the Publishers Clearing House Sweepstakes every year. We really go for it. We do our homework. We play hardball. We keep our eyes on the bottom line. We always lose.

"I think this year we should leverage our options," I said when the Publishers Clearing House Million Dollar Sweeps entry arrived in the mail a couple of months ago.

"What does that mean?" my younger daughter, Sarah, asked.

"Your mother can explain the details," I said. "I'm strictly an idea man."

I'm the one who had the idea about entering sweepstakes in the first place. Sarah, who is eleven, hasn't come up with any sound investment strategies since she got stymied trying to fill out the entry form for a drawing some beer company was holding for a new Pontiac Trans Am ("What should I put for business phone?"). It's natural for me to have a lot of ideas about these matters because I know a number of Wall Street millionaires. As it happens, every single person in the lower third of my college class — every single person, that is, except Blinko Moshler, who's a prominent lawyer in Toledo, and Dalt Durfee, who is the Deputy Undersecretary of State for Asian Economic Affairs — is a Wall Street millionaire. I occasionally run into one of them, usually at some restaurant I can't really afford. They're always talking about leveraging their options, or maybe optioning their leverages; ask my wife if you want the details.

They also talk a lot about what they're getting out of and what they're getting into. "I just got out of the market and into shrimp boats," one of the millionaires said when I came across a brace of them at an East Side nouvelle cuisine joint that seemed to be charging the price of a shrimp boat for three cold shrimp and a heart-shaped raspberry.

"I just got out of shrimp boats and into boxcars," said the other one, someone I'll call Martin G. Cashflow. In his crowd, Cashflow is known for having just got out of whatever it is that everyone else is about to get into. Cashflow also happens to be one of those trendy millionaires who gets in and out of fads at the same time he's getting in and out of investments, so sometimes he's getting out of backgammon and into cattle ranches or into Sufism and out of discount plumbing supplies. Cashflow is the person who told me a long time ago that my problem was that writers are labor in a labor-intensive industry.

"I just got out of the New York State Instant Lotto and into the Reader's Digest Sweepstakes," I said. When they looked unimpressed, I assured them that I was savvy enough to have marked my entry form in a way that kept my name in the sweepstakes without obligating me to sign up at the special sweepstakes rate for a subscription to *Reader's Digest* for life plus ninety-nine years. I don't subscribe to any magazines. Some time after Cashflow told me that my problem was being labor in a labor-intensive industry, he told me that the smart money got out of magazines and into software years ago, at around the same time he got out of silver futures and into the Maharaj Ji. ("I don't think I want to get into software," I said at the time, thinking that it had something to do with flannel pajamas. "Kid, you *are* software," Cashflow replied. "That's your problem.") I figured there was nothing much I could do about writing for magazines — unless, of course, the big New Jersey Lottery number does turn out one year to be my Army serial number with the last two digits reversed for good luck — but I was at least smart enough not to subscribe to any.

This year, we had a family meeting about the Publishers Clearing House Sweepstakes. We sat at the dining room table, with sharpened pencils and clean white memo pads in front of us. "How's the little-bitty sticker end holding up, Sarah?" I asked. In our operation, Sarah is the specialist in how to figure out which little-bitty sticker is supposed to be pasted where on the entry blank.

"Piece of cake," Sarah said.

With Sarah trouble-shooting the little-bitty sticker end, I figured, the main decision we had facing us was which of the three superprizes we wanted — a certified check for $250,000, a $250,000 custom-built dream home, or $40,000 a year for ten years.

"How do the numbers look on that one, Abigail?" I asked my older daughter.

"Ten times forty thousand is four hundred thousand, Daddy," Abigail said. "Don't you remember what I told you about just adding a zero on the tens table?"

"But the question is whether we want to go for the ten-year payout or get the two-fifty up front and put that money to work for us," I said.

"I'd rather have a Pontiac Trans Am," Sarah said.

"O.K., we'll meet again as soon as I figure out which option gives us the most leverage," I said, trying to imagine how Martin Cashflow would end a meeting. "I'll have my girl get back to your girl."

"But Daddy," Abigail said, "we *are* your girls."

I spent the next weeks trying to answer the questions that would allow us to eyeball a ballpark figure on the bottom line, or something like that. Is a $250,000 custom-built dream home the sort of thing Cashflow has in mind when he goes on about shelters? Aren't all $250,000 dream homes custom-built, or do some people have prefabricated dreams? In ten years, will $40,000 buy a Pontiac Trans Am? How about a Mars bar? I was thinking about such questions when Alice pointed out that entries to the Publishers Clearing House Sweepstakes had been due four days before ("You forgot to assign someone the deadline end"). I still had questions. If we decided to take the up-front cash and get it working for us, how many Instant Lotto tickets would $250,000 buy? What could "leverage your options" possibly mean?

Urban Mass Transit

April 2, 1983

IN ITS COVERAGE of a railroad strike that forced
Westchester County commuters to take the subway
from the Bronx, the *New York Times* ran a headline
recently that said "Rail Commuters Learn the ABC's
of the IRT." The headline writer who did that one is
obviously someone who lives in Montclair, New Jersey,
commutes every day to the Port Authority bus terminal,
and walks the three blocks to the *Times*. If he had
ever tried riding the subways, he would know that the
IRT doesn't have any ABCs. It has &% #s, and even
those are illegible. Any Westchester commuter who
tries to go from the Bronx to midtown Manhattan
thinking he can learn the ABCs of the IRT is going to
end up in Queens Plaza. Most people who try to get
from the Bronx to midtown Manhattan end up in
Queens Plaza anyway, but at least they do not travel
under any illusions.

Many years ago, I revealed the secret of the New

York subway system: the secret of finding your way around in it is actually a secret. That's right. There are things about the subways that you are not meant to know. One of the things is how to get from the Bronx to midtown. You don't believe me? Ask yourself why the New York subway system, alone among the mass transit systems of the world, has maps inside rather than outside the trains. It's to force you to get on the wrong train in order to find out where you're going. Then you have to shove your way through a lot of people who look irritable and maybe dangerous to find a map upon which no one has spray-painted "Rico-179." Then, assuming that you are a graduate of the Royal Institute of Cartography, you decipher the map to discover that the first step in reaching your destination is to get off the wrong train at the next stop. Fine. The next stop is Queens Plaza.

When the *Times* headline writer implied that the IRT has ABCs, he might have been thinking of the BMT, which doesn't have ABCs but does have RRs and Ns. Although you wouldn't know it from the dissimilarity of the letters, the RR train and the N train go to more or less the same places. Why do they go to more or less the same places? Because you wouldn't know it from the dissimilarity of the letters, that's why. That is also why the D and the QB go to more or less the same places. In keeping with the same policy, the A and the AA, which sound very similar indeed, do not go to more or less the same places. Why? You were not meant to know.

Why were you not meant to know? Because you're an out-of-towner, that's why. The whole point of the subway system is to keep out-of-towners — particularly out-of-towners who have lived in New York for twenty or thirty years — from finding their way around. Only real New Yorkers can find their way around in the subway. If just anybody could find his way around in the subway, there wouldn't be any distinction in being a real New Yorker except talking funny.

I'm an out-of-towner myself, although I try to hide it sometimes by talking knowingly of the QB or the GG, neither of which I would dare ride. Once, while going uptown on the West Side IRT local, I was waiting for the doors to close at the Fourteenth Street station when a voice on the public address system announced that the train on the local track was going to become an *East Side* train, making express stops only. I dashed from the train. Safe on the platform, I looked back. No one else had moved. I couldn't believe it. Didn't anybody else know how inconvenient an East Side express train might be for somebody who started out on the West Side local? Suddenly, it hit me: Why had the announcement been understandable? Normally, public address announcements on the subway are so unintelligible that for years I wasn't sure which language they were being made in. As the doors closed, a real New Yorker sitting on the train gave me a knowing smile. It must have all been a feint to shake up the out-of-towners. I had been spotted.

Knowledge of feints may be why New Yorkers seem

so docile in the face of the unscheduled stops and bizarre route changes of public conveyances. A few years ago, the *Times* reported that, according to a survey taken by the staff of a state assemblyman, almost all buses arrived at their final stop late and 14 percent did not arrive at all. Never! I think of those buses often. At the first detour — a sharp left from Madison Avenue straight across town through the Lincoln Tunnel — the passengers must have assumed that the driver was just having a bit of fun with a Japanese tourist. They would look up briefly, and then go back to their *New York Posts*. But how about now? I see a bus somewhere on the plains of Nebraska. The driver is hunched over the wheel, wearing the demonic look of someone who cracked under the strain of being asked 238 times in one day how far up Madison Avenue the Number 3 goes. By now, the passengers have been reduced to reading the horoscope section and the ads for singles weekends in the Poconos. The only sound is the voice of a lady in the back, who says, "Does this bus stop in Bay Ridge or doesn't it?"

Keeping out-of-towners confused is why New Yorkers are always saying the subways are dangerous. The subways are not dangerous. Buckingham Palace and Beverly Hills are both more dangerous than the subways. Thinking that the subways are dangerous keeps out-of-towners too edgy to find their way around. Say an out-of-towner on his way from Herald Square to Bloomingdale's on the N train sees two suspicious-looking teen-agers get on at Times Square. He thinks they're muggers because they're wearing sneakers. Actually, they're honor students at Brooklyn Tech. They're wearing sneakers because they're both champion high jumpers as well as honor students, and whenever they go to midtown they like to entertain themselves by high-jumping over telephone booths. The out-of-towner keeps looking at them out of the corner of his eye. He is concentrating so hard he doesn't notice that the train has stopped at Bloomingdale's and then stopped again. Suddenly realizing his mistake, he rushes from the train at the next stop. Queens Plaza.

Seder Splitsville

April 23, 1983

F OR US, the saddest news of the spring holiday season was that our old friends the Levines decided to get a divorce, citing irreconcilable differences over what kind of Passover seder to attend. It seems only yesterday that we were all together at the Levines for a Freedom Seder — asking that all people oppressed by antidemocratic dictators be freed as the Jews were freed from Pharaoh's grasp, debating the issue of whether the Pharaoh's daughter was trying to co-opt Moses by hauling him out of the bulrushes, and tucking away some of Linda Levine's superb gefilte fish done with a simple béchamel sauce. But when Richie Levine and I had a drink together to talk about the split-up he reminded me that the Freedom Seder was almost twenty years ago. Since then, he told me, the Levines have observed Passover at dinners that included an Environmental Seder that emphasized the effect the parting of the Red Sea might have had on marine life and a seder done entirely in Reformation dress. It shows you how time flies.

When we had our drink, Richie was in a reflective mood, talking about the seders he used to go to as a kid in Detroit at the home of his Uncle Mo the Gonif. Richie happened to have two uncles named Mo — one of them a failed actor who lived off his relatives, the other a prosperous businessman who had once been accused of embezzlement by his partner — and to keep them straight, the family called them Uncle Mo the Schnorrer and Uncle Mo the Gonif.

"Those were the days," Richie said. "My sisters and I would get a little tipsy on the Passover wine and kid Aunt Sarah about the matzoh balls being kind of rubbery: 'I'll just save this one, thanks, Aunt Sarah; we're going to play jacks a little later, and it'll make a good ball.'"

"Simpler times, Richie," I said. "Those were simpler times."

It was Harold the Committed, our neighborhood causemeister, who organized the Freedom Seder at the Levines, but Richie didn't seem to blame him for anything that followed. "Hal the C's O.K.," Richie said. "Sure, I got a little bored when he went into that long spiel comparing Moses' brother Aaron to Che Guevara, but I figured it wasn't much different from when I got restless waiting for Uncle Mo the Gonif to stumble through all that Hebrew so that I could have another go at the Manischewitz burgundy. Times change."

I nodded, and looked into my drink for a while. "So what went wrong, then?" I finally said.

"Well, nothing right away," Richie said. "Harold the Committed wasn't in town for Passover for a few years there; that's when he was going to Sweden every spring to do that ecumenical Unilateral Disarmament Seder with the schismatic Lutheran peaceniks. Josh and Jenny weren't old enough then to know what was going on, so I guess we just skipped Passover for quite a while, except for that Interfaith Seder at the Mohlers' where we saw you — the one where the priest got blotto and the Methodist minister fainted into the chopped liver."

I remembered the occasion well. The priest polished off the Passover wine supply so quickly that the last two blessings had to be said over apple juice. The Methodist minister started in on the chopped liver with considerable gusto — having had up to that moment no way at all of knowing that he carried in his bloodstream antibodies that would set off a violent chemical reaction to schmaltz.

Apparently, when the kids got old enough to understand what Passover was — Josh was about six and Jenny four — Richie assumed there would simply be a regular family seder every year, but Linda, who had always been intense about causes, was convinced that a seder had to be a statement. After she lost interest in national liberation and gourmet cooking, the Levines went to the Environmental Seder, which Richie remembered as having been "mostly about microorganisms." That flowed into a Natural Foods Seder, whose symbolism irritated Richie. "I mean, let's face it," he told me. "The mortar that the Jews made in Egypt didn't look anything like mung beans, and it's silly to pretend it did."

"So that's what did it?" I asked. "The mung beans for mortar?"

"Oh, no," Richie said. "That was years ago. After that — let me see — we had a seder at a radical feminist collective where they refused to recognize the killing of the Egyptians' first-born sons as a curse, which made Josh feel a little uncomfortable of course."

"So you said you wouldn't go back there the next year?"

"No, no. The next year we went to a seder where the guest of honor was an Indian holy man Linda's pals were very big on at the time. He went on and on about whether plain matzoh had inner peace. Finally I told him I'd promise to stay away from his ashram if he'd stay away from my seders — sort of a reverse interfaith arrangement."

"So that did it?"

"No. What did it is when Linda got involved in finding her roots, and we started going to seders every year in Brooklyn with Hasidim who pray in Hebrew for six or eight hours before you can have a bite of gefilte fish. I have a lot of respect for those people, but they're not the sort of crowd that goes for matzoh-ball jokes. So this year, I told Linda that if we're searching so hard for roots, my roots are in Detroit: I was going to seder at Uncle Mo the Gonif's. So she said go. It was great. Uncle Mo the Gonif and Aunt Sarah are getting on, but one of my sisters helped with the cooking, and she even knows how to make those bouncy matzoh balls. Uncle Mo the Gonif's Hebrew hasn't improved. He's really a very sweet man, my Uncle Mo the Gonif — as long as you don't leave him alone with the books."

"I hope there's no acrimony between you and Linda," I said.

"It's a very amicable separation," Richie said. "The only problem we're having is who gets custody of the kids on Passover."

would drive the best chefs off to Hong Kong where you might be able to get at them."

So? It's true that when the Red Guards inspired Harold the Committed to pass out leaflets saying "Export the Revolution!" I was saying "Export the Recipes!" So what? So what if my daughter prefers chocolate to anarchosyndicalism? I reminded Harold of a few great quotations — "Enlightened self-interest is the cornerstone of democracy," for instance, and "The sins of the ice cream cone are not visited upon the father" — but he seems unimpressed.

"You are not a serious person," he said as he examined a piece of bean curd and then launched into an explanation of the role soybeans might play in making the Third World agriculturally self-sufficient.

I didn't want to say anything to that — my mouth happened to be full — but I was surprised that Harold the Committed had already forgotten the serious political commitment I had displayed only weeks before while I was downing shashlik at one of the Brighton Beach restaurants the recent Russian immigrants have opened and discussing how to find out which of the new Greek places in Astoria was worth trying. "You will find nobody more passionate in his support of the liberalization of immigration laws than I am," I had said. "Let the Russians in — particularly if we can find some who have a slightly lighter touch with dumplings! Let the Greeks in! Certainly let the Italians in! Let most of Thailand in! I will resist with every fiber in my being any attempt to go back to the racist quota system that for so long kept a decent supply of stuffed paratha and chicken vindaloo from these shores!"

Talk about commitment! Where was Harold when the immigration laws were changed to give priority to reuniting families and I began looking for people willing to sign affidavits swearing that they were blood relatives of the six top *crabes farcis* cooks in Martinique?

"You are callous about the fate of baby seals," Harold said, as he passed me the pan-fried flounder.

"That's not a very nice thing to say to somebody, Hal the C," I said between bites. If there's pressure on the seal herd, as the environmentalists would put it, it's not of my doing. The only seal recipe I ever heard of was brought back from Greenland by a linguist studying Eskimo dialects. It began, "Kill and gut one seal, fill the body cavity with auks, bury in sand, dig up in six months." That's not the sort of thing likely to transform me into someone who is always storming into the butcher shop (or would it be the fish market?) to demand a steady supply of seal. "I'm innocent of seal demand, Hal the C," I said. "If you start talking about lessening the pressure on the Peking duck flock, of course, that's another story."

Before Harold could accuse me of being an extinctionist, I assured him I would be in the forefront of any movement to make certain that there are enough Peking ducks to make more Peking ducks; they are born, as I understand it, wrapped in a pancake that also includes scallions, celery, and hoisin sauce. It's only reasonable, though, to have priorities in these matters. If someone came to me and said, "The Jell-O mold as we know it is threatened with extinction," I would not rush to the barricades. I wouldn't lift a finger to save whatever beast it is that produces Surf 'n' Turf, a dish popular in the sort of phony, overpriced restaurants that under a more enlightened immigration policy will eventually be replaced by Sicilian fish houses and Cambodian noodle shops. (The surfnturf, as I have always envisioned it, is a tiny, aquatic Hereford that has horns and a shell — a beast that moves through the depths slowly, in herds, and can both moo and draw flies under water.)

"I've heard that during the American adventure in Vietnam there were a lot of nights when you watched Julia Child reruns instead of the war," Harold said.

Was I in a Chinese restaurant or a Pol Pot re-education camp? Whatever happened to the days when what we discussed in Chinatown was whether the braised fish at the next table looked better than what we were having? Also, that happened to be a low blow. I watched the war. I was tuned in for the entire conflict. I was concerned. I was reacting. When Saigon fell and American helicopters hovered above the desperate crowd of people trying to escape from the embassy compound, I was the one who sat in front of his television set and shouted, "Get the chefs! Get the chefs!"

Are we talking about environmentalism? Then who was it who wanted to save part of the earth's irreplaceable supply of natural gas by mandating that all barbecue joints cook on real hickory wood? Are we talking about anticolonialism? Who has been the person most vocal in his denunciation of the British Empire's effort to impose on untold millions of Third World people its belief that vegetables must be kept boiling as long as Parliament is in session?

"The world could be destroyed any moment by a nuclear holocaust," Harold the Committed said.

"That's true, Hal the C," I said, reaching for a platter. "So it's silly to leave any of this lo mein."

Not Loony

June 25, 1983

I READ IN the *New York Times* recently that Edward
C. Schmults is not crazy. A citizen's simply enjoying
the state of sanity is not usually considered news —
ordinarily, I suppose, you'd have to take out an ad to
nose that sort of thing around — but Schmults happens to be Deputy Attorney General of the United
States, and, I realized as I was reading the *Times* piece
on him, it's becoming common for the press to consider the sanity of a Reagan Administration official
newsworthy. An assistant secretary of state who has
doubts about whether the United States was created by
God to win the world for Jesus through nuclear weap-
onry and doesn't subscribe without qualification to the
international monetary theories of Adolphe Menjou
can find himself discussed in the morning paper. I've
seen newspaper reports of James Baker's sanity now
and then. They're couched in indirect terms, of course;
the headline does not say "White House Aide Thought

Sane." The story on Schmults took the same approach. The headline said "Justice Aide Makes Mark as Mediator," but it was obvious that the discerning reader was meant to interpret that as "Top Justice Aide Widely Considered Not Loony."

You'd think that by now the stories on Baker's sanity would be presented in the form of what newspapers sometimes call an update — "No Change in Baker's Mental Condition," maybe, or "Reagan Aide Still Thought Sane" — but that's not the way they're handled. In the first place, it is customary to discuss the mental state of important government officials with euphemisms. In the story about Schmults, for instance, his style is contrasted with Attorney General William French Smith's "shy manner and cautious pronouncements." That's a complicated euphemism. It may mean "lightweight"; on the other hand, it may mean "backward lightweight."

In Baker's case, the euphemism is "pragmatic." Whenever you read that someone in the Reagan Administration is pragmatic, what you're really being told is that he is not crazy. Reporters have their ways of gauging such things. Let's say, for instance, that a new wizard of supply-side economics is received at the White House to demonstrate his theory that poverty can be eliminated simply by eliminating all tax on capital gains — a theory he illustrates with an impressive array of graphs, even though his performance is marred a bit by his tendency to twitch uncontrollably at times and by the fact that he is costumed as the French dauphin — and, at the end of the presentation, James Baker says, "Are you sure it will work?" Pragmatism.

Why is it necessary to use a euphemism for an admirable quality such as sanity? Simple: among the most zealous Reagan supporters, sanity is not assumed to be an admirable quality. It's not as bad as poverty, but it's not great. That's why the congressmen interviewed for the story I saw in the *Times* expressed concern that they might damage Schmults's reputation in the Administration by saying that they consider him a sensible and straightforward man. I wouldn't be surprised, in fact, if some of the President's most zealous supporters believe that reporters are protecting sanity suspects like Schmults by using euphemisms and that such protection is just one more confirmation that the media is controlled by a cabal of left-wingers. But that's crazy, you say? My point precisely.

Reporters are human beings, though, and they presumably give some consideration to the human consequences when they start turning up evidence that a previously untainted member of the Administration may be flat-out rational. Even in the heat of the chase — a pair of those relentless post-Watergate snoops on the trail of some assistant secretary of state — it must be apparent what effect an exposé could have on the quarry's career and on his family. ("Joey's dad's a pragmatist — nah, nah, nah.")

I see the two snoops huddled in the city room. The

hardnosed Woodbern has a look of triumph on his face (except for his nose, which stays hard whatever his expression). "We've got him nailed," he says. "I found out that he was on the board of a hospital that didn't turn down federal aid for its emergency room."

"I guess we should go with it," says Wardstein, the more sensitive of the two, but he looks troubled. He knows what can happen to an Administration official who finds himself under suspicion of sanity. "Are you sure we don't have anything on the other side?" he asks his partner. "Doesn't he even believe in the existence of the Illuminati conspiracy? Isn't it possible that he's a follower of Ayn Rand or Billy James Hargis? Is it really balanced reporting to say he's balanced?"

"Are you getting soft, Wardstein?" Woodbern says, looming forward in a way that makes him seem to be brandishing his adamantine sniffer.

"O.K., let's go with it," Wardstein finally says, but as the presses roll his thoughts dwell on the assistant secretary's fate. He can see the man quietly emptying his desk at State while his loyal secretary sniffles in the outer office. "He's the last person I would have suspected," she says to the security man who waits quietly at the door. "Why, only last week he said that the way to control arms is to build a space death-ray, and when those nice men came to lecture us on how the Russians caused the mud slides in Utah with ultrasonics, he nodded very politely."

As the assistant secretary passes his secretary, he pauses, and smiles. Then he puts his thumbs in his ears, wiggles his fingers, crosses his eyes, and sticks out his tongue. She smiles. Then, as he leaves with the security guard, she looks down at the newspaper on her desk, and starts sniffling again. The headline says "Reagan Aide Thought Sane."

Mo.

July 23, 1983

MY RESPONSE to the news of a campaign to promote the proper pronunciation of Missouri is simple: it's about time. We Missourians have suffered enough. Yes, we have suffered. I know what you're saying. You're saying, "Big deal!" Don't deny it. You're saying, "Why is he getting all excited just because somebody pronounced his silly state wrong?" A rhetorical question meant as an insult! No? Then why did you say "*silly state*"? As you Easterners are always saying, was that really an accident? Was it really an accident that you didn't say, "Why is he getting all excited just because somebody pronounced his proud and historically significant state wrong?" Even if Missouri were a silly state — and it is most emphatically not, despite years of being mispronounced and having Missouri mule jokes told about it — that would be no excuse to mispronounce it. If we mispronounced everything we considered silly, this place would be a shambles. Democratic congressmen would rise in the House to criticize Secretary of the Interior James Wutt as the silliest man in the Roogan Administration. We can't have that.

Now you're wondering how Missouri is pronounced. All of a sudden, after all these years, you want to know how Missouri is pronounced. I'm tempted to say, "It's not a matter that need concern you." That would be petty, though, and if there's one thing we Missourians have avoided through all of this it's pettiness — although, believe me, we have been sorely tempted. Missoura. That's how it's pronounced — as if it were spelled Missoura. Until I was about twelve, I didn't just pronounce it as if it were spelled Missoura, I spelled it as if it were spelled Missoura. Nobody ever corrected me. The teacher must have thought it was spelled that way, too.

Now you're going to say that Missourians aren't very good spellers. Go ahead. Say it. Then I'll say, "How about Harry S Truman?" He was from Missouri, and he could spell rings around the fellow they have in there now. Harry S Truman could spell so well that he knew not to put a period after his middle initial. Why not? Because it didn't stand for anything, that's why. His name wasn't Harry Sebastian Truman or anything like that. We don't name people names like that in Missouri. The S in Harry S Truman just stood for S — that is considered a fine middle name in Missouri — and you don't put a period after an initial if it stands for itself. That's the sort of punctuational subtlety you learn in Missouri schools. Harry S Truman always said

Mo.

"Missoura." I don't know how he spelled it, but he could spell it any way he wanted to, because he was the President.

I can hear what you're saying, even though you're halfway mumbling it because you're afraid I'll get mad and threaten to punch you in the nose the way Harry S Truman threatened that music critic who insulted his daughter. (The Missouri position on that incident, by the way, is this: the man was a yellow dog and deserved to be dealt with.) You're saying, "Calm down." Speak up! I'm not going to punch you in the nose. Through all of this, we Missourians have avoided violence — although, let's face it, what would *you* do if some Eastern pantywaist who had just made a mad-dog pronunciational attack on *your* proud and historically significant state told *you* to calm down? Punch him in the nose?

I think I could have remained calm all these years if our suffering had consisted simply of hearing uninformed people mispronounce Missouri. There's more to it than that. They not only mispronounce Missouri — they make fun of us for pronouncing it correctly. If a Missourian who happens to be in the East pronounces his own state correctly, you can count on somebody saying, "Oh, I suppose folks out there pronounce it Missoura — heh, heh." It's that "heh, heh" that tempts us to violence.

I know what you're saying. You're saying, "He seems to be just a tad defensive." You'd say, "He seems to be just a tad defensive — heh, heh," except you're afraid

· 133 ·

if you said that I'd punch you in the nose. Yes, I'm a tad defensive. You'd be defensive too if a lot of Easterners said "heh, heh" at you for correctly pronouncing your own state. That's not all they do. They pronounce a lot of other words in a way that keeps Missourians from knowing what's going on. Take that fad Alex Haley started by tracing his family way back to some place where nobody ever heard of cornbread. People on television kept saying they were interested in tracing their roots — as if it rhymed with lutes or suits — and for the longest time people in Missouri who never heard it pronounced that way thought the fad was about tracing highway routes. The fad was practically over before Missourians figured out that what was being discussed was roots — which in Missouri is pronounced to rhyme with toots, just like it's spelled. Once Missouri people put away their road maps and started tracing their roots, of course, they found them to be proud and historically significant.

What campaign? Is that what you're saying — what campaign to promote the correct pronunciation of Missouri? The campaign that just took out an advertisement in the Lee's Summit, Mo., *Journal* exhorting all true Missourians to fight the conspiracy of TV broadcasters, "tradition-trampling educators and their follow-the-leader ventriloquist dummies" and other assorted dog-buckets who are trying to blot out the proper pronunciation of Missouri through "un-American censorship, persecution, and brainwashing." I don't know who wrote the advertisement, but I admire his style. I'm with him. All the way. All right, I'm a little uneasy about his asking parents to report any teacher who has "made a mockery of the First Amendment and the Golden Rule" by requiring children to use the "parrot squeaky, long-e Missouree" pronunciation, but, as they say in Missouri, you can't make an omelet without Kraft cheese. His scholarship is impressive, although don't look up the ad in the hope of finding out why a state that is properly pronounced Missoura has a parrot-squeaky spelling. It's not a matter that need concern you.

Bonjour, Madame

———

WHEN I READ *Newsweek*'s July 11 cover story on what the world thinks of America and Americans, I happened to be in France, so I naturally took advantage of my morning croissant run to check out the *Newsweek* findings.

"*Bonjour, monsieur*," Madame LeBlanc, who runs the bakery, said as I walked in the door.

"*Bonjour, madame*," I said. "Tell me, Madame Le-Blanc, what do you think of us Americans at this stage of history?"

Madame LeBlanc looked at me silently for a while, as if considering her response. Finally, she said, "*Comment?*"

"Don't be afraid to speak up," I said. "It's all for research."

Madame LeBlanc looked blank.

"I know you Europeans think we Americans worry too much about what other people think of us, Madame

· 136 ·

LeBlanc," I said. "But if we need an example of the problems caused by false impressions of national traits, we need look no further than Maurice Chevalier."

"Maurice Chevalier?" Madame LeBlanc said. Her eyes shot toward the door, and then she peered over my shoulder as if checking to see if someone was standing behind me. "*N'est-il pas mort?*"

"For years, the impression most Americans had of French people was based on Maurice Chevalier," I explained. "So they expected every Frenchman they met to be a charming, debonair old gent who at any moment might start singing 'Sank Evan for leetle gerls.' Naturally, they were disappointed when they came to France and the Frenchmen they met were sour customs officers with scratchy pens and some nasty Parisian cabdriver who pretended not to understand their French when they said '*Bonjour.*' "

"*Ah, bonjour, monsieur*," Madame LeBlanc said, smiling at me in her accustomed way.

"Oh. *Bonjour, madame*," I said. "As I was saying, American tourists were very disappointed to discover that the only Frenchman who acted like Maurice Chevalier was Maurice Chevalier — and he was in California. So they started going to Italy, where they could still run into somebody now and then who acted like Ezio Pinza, and you fellows lost a bunch of money."

Madame LeBlanc seemed to remember suddenly that the countertop of her display case needed dusting.

"So," I continued, "if a French magazine did a similar survey (although I realize you people don't do that

sort of thing; it would be what General DeGaulle used
to call 'uncool'), you would probably find out that the
reason so many Americans think of the French as
petty, mean-spirited functionaries . . . although, God
knows, that's not the way I think of you and Monsieur
LeBlanc, Madame LeBlanc — you with your ever-
present smile and your cheerful *bonjour* —"

"*Bonjour, monsieur*," Madame LeBlanc said, putting
down her feather duster.

"*Bonjour, madame.* What I'm really asking is
whether you include yourself among those French
people who find us Americans industrious, energetic,
inventive, decisive, and friendly. I don't mean to muddy
the sample here, Madame LeBlanc, but I might point
out that it's pretty industrious and energetic for someone who's supposed to be on vacation to present himself right in front of your display case every morning
at eight-thirty on the dot, friendly as a puppydog,
and I must say that a certain amount of inventiveness
was required to discover the baker in town who used
the quantity of butter we Americans associate with a
week's supply for a family of four in every one of his
croissants —"

"*Croissants, monsieur?*" Madame LeBlanc said,
reaching for the door of the display case.

"Precisely, Madame LeBlanc," I said. "And I would
like to say, concerning *Newsweek*'s finding that the
French do not associate Americans with honesty, that
the little misunderstanding we had last week about
whether it was a ten-franc piece or a twenty-centime

piece you gave me in my change was just that — a misunderstanding. Ours is a young culture, Madame LeBlanc, and we're still not real good with old money."

Madame LeBlanc turned from the counter and ducked into the room where the croissants are baked by Monsieur LeBlanc — a petty, mean-spirited functionary I would rate high in industriousness, energy, and butter content.

"Madame LeBlanc!" I called after her. "Madame LeBlanc! I know *Newsweek* found that a lot of French people think having Americans around increases the chance of war, but I'd like to remind you that the question was about American *military* presence. Surely, Madame LeBlanc, a misunderstanding over small change would not lead you to confuse me with some hopped-up G.I. who might decide to lay a ground-to-ground on Leipzig just to put a little zip into a Saturday night . . ."

There was no sound from behind the curtain. I stood silently, wondering whether it would have been appropriate for me to explain that I had nothing whatever to do with the American pop culture that the French people surveyed by *Newsweek* considered so influential. Finally, Madame LeBlanc emerged from the back room. She stood in her accustomed place behind the counter, and looked at me as if I had just walked into the shop.

"*Bonjour, monsieur,*" she said, in her usual cheerful tone.

"*Bonjour, madame,*" I said.

"*Qu'est-ce que vous voulez aujourd'hui, monsieur?*"

"I would like to say, Madame LeBlanc, that when it comes to this Star Wars mickey mouse, not to speak of the Mickey Mouse mickey mouse, I have nothing —"

"*Croissants, monsieur? Brioches? Pains au chocolat?*"

"Nine croissants, *s'il vous plaît*," I said, holding up nine fingers.

"*Très bien, monsieur,*" Madame LeBlanc said, with considerable enthusiasm.

"I notice that you seem to admire my decisiveness," I said, gathering up my croissants. "It's a national trait."

Pinkos at Rest

———

October 8, 1983

WHY, I HAVE BEEN ASKED, does *The Nation* choose
to publish only every other week in July and August
even though the oppression of the downtrodden goes
on every day of the year? The question was raised this
summer in a rather strongly worded letter that a reader
named Sheldon A. Schryer apparently meant for the
entire *Nation* staff but sent to me — perhaps because
he remembered my name from the time a year or so
ago when he chastised me for allowing the torment of
the Scottsboro Boys to slip from my memory.

"Enemies of the people!" Schryer began. "Lackeys
of the Bosses! Pisherkehs! Or have I missed something? Could it be that the unionbusting racists who
run Southern textile mills treat their workers with respect and brotherhood on alternate weeks in July?
Are the political prisoners who rot in the jails of fascist
dictators in South America permitted during the summer months to alternate a week of freedom with every

week in the torture chambers? Or, to put it another way, is it possible for editors and writers to fight oppression one week and spend the next week in beach houses sipping gin and tonics (made with limes picked by nonunion braceros)? Is it possible that political commitment can be turned off and on, like alternate-side-of-the-street parking regulations?"

I thought Schryer had raised some interesting questions about *Nation* policy, but I was not, of course, the person to answer them. At *The Nation*, I am simply a part-time columnist — doing what the people who attempt to organize those Southern textile mills would refer to as piecework. I don't want to appear to be distancing myself from an institution while it's under intense criticism, but I might point out that I don't even have an office at *The Nation* — any more than the bent but seemingly indefatigable immigrants who did piecework in their Lower East Side tenements maintained offices in, say, the Triangle Shirtwaist Company. Schryer's letter, in fact, reached me in Nova Scotia, where my family and I have spent our summers ever since I discovered that Canada is a country in which the New Hampshire primary is almost never mentioned.

Confident that *The Nation*'s editor, one Victor S. Navasky, could provide some persuasive answers to Schryer's questions, I telephoned the *Nation* office in New York. The telephone rang for a very long time. Finally, it was answered by a *Nation* employee I'll call Emile Zola.

"What's the latest on government surveillance, oil company profiteering, and the oppression of the poor, Zola?" I said, to make conversation. "I don't get much news up here."

"I don't know," Zola said. "We don't publish this week. I'm only in here because it's air-conditioned."

I asked to speak to Victor S. Navasky. "It's about policy," I added.

"He isn't here," Zola said. "He's in England."

England? "I guess he's exposing dreadful working conditions in the Yorkshire textile industry," I said.

"I don't think so," Zola said. "He got a grant to go over there and talk to his friends, although I don't think it was worded quite like that. He didn't say anything about going to Yorkshire, and he asked me about a couple of restaurants in Hampstead."

I figured the publisher would be in a position to discuss policy, so I asked for Hamilton Fish 3rd. Don't ask me why a left-wing magazine has a publisher with two last names and a number. I don't even have an office there.

"He isn't here either," Zola said. "He's been gone most of the summer — to Third World countries."

"Which Third World country is he in?"

"Mexico," Zola said.

"You mean going to Acapulco is visiting a Third World country?" I asked, noticing as I said it that I had adopted Schryer's interrogatory style.

"I don't know if Acapulco is where he is," Zola said. "He didn't leave an address."

Was it possible that Hamilton Fish 3rd was drinking margaritas in Zihuatanejo or Cuernavaca and calling it a visit to the Third World? Could it be that he was a traitor to *this* class, too? Was he some sort of double agent?

Not having any idea how to reach Hamilton Fish 3rd, I decided to wait for Navasky's return from England. I phoned around the middle of August, and, after a number of rings, Zola answered again.

"You missed him," Zola said, before I could ask if South America was still rife with dictators and the arms race continued to threaten mankind. "He was here for a day or two, but now he's on Martha's Vineyard."

Martha's Vineyard! I figured that Navasky was back at work. Martha's Vineyard, the summer home of a lot of left-wing intellectuals, is also known as the single most difficult place on the Atlantic coast for a non-property-owner to get to the beach — a place where renowned writers of a progressive bent use their gifts to compose No Trespassing signs. I could imagine Navasky in the thick of the story — interviewing disgruntled day-trippers who had been driven off the beach at gunpoint by civil liberties lawyers and contributors to the *New York Review of Books*, burrowing in courthouse records to find instances of scallop fishermen being snookered out of their land by neo-Keynesian economists.

"I suppose he's up there exposing the hypocrisy of the Landed Left," I said to Zola.

"Not unless he's trying to embarrass them by showing up at all their cocktail parties," Zola said.

Well, that left no question about what I should write to Schryer. "Apologist!" I began. "Protector of Backsliders! Moderate! Or could it be that South American dictators take the entire summer off? Is warmongering seasonal? Is apartheid in force only during the academic year? Could it be that from June through August it is not important to remember the torment of the Scottsboro Boys?"

Marc Rich and I
at Camp Osceola

———

October 29, 1983
AS IT HAPPENS, I went to Boy Scout camp with Marc
Rich. That's right. Who's Marc Rich? Is that what you
said? The question, if I may so, reveals an abysmal
ignorance of world affairs. Marc Rich happens to be
the reclusive, enigmatic, fabulously wealthy commodities trader who was just accused by the government
of flimflamming it out of forty-eight million in taxes
and is now believed to be hiding out in Zug, Switzer-
land, or maybe Spain. That's who. I went to Boy Scout
camp with him, in Missouri. In 1949. We lived in the
same tent. The name of the camp was Camp Osceola,
B.S.A. It was where Boy Scouts from Kansas City went
to camp. I can tell that you don't believe any of this.

One reason you don't believe it is that you think I
make things up. I do make things up — I made up that
thing about Ronald Reagan's son shouting "Hiya, Dad!"
to a man on Fifth Avenue who turned out to be Joel

McCrea — but I didn't make this up. The other reason
you don't believe me is that all of the stories you've
read about Marc Rich talk about how he came to this
country with his family from Europe during the war
and grew up in Brooklyn with his friend Pincus
(Pinky) Green — also a fabulously wealthy commodities trader now, although only marginally enigmatic — and life as a Kansas City Boy Scout doesn't
fit your picture of the young Marc trading some Bor-
ough Park candy store owner one used Batman comic
for enough egg creams to float the entire stickball
team. All of the stories you've read, that is, unless you
happened to read the story in the *Kansas City Times*
on October 5 which revealed that before moving to
Brooklyn, Marc Rich's family lived in Kansas City for
six years ("Mr. Rich's life-style apparently was nurtured in Kansas City, where he spent his formative
years, investigators said") and that for two years Marc
went to Southwest High School, which is where I went,
and where, as long as we're on the subject, David
Douglas Duncan went, and also Charlie Black, who
played basketball for the University of Kansas. The
Kansas City Times did not reveal the Camp Osceola
angle. I'm revealing that now. Marc Rich and I were
at Osceola together. Not Pincus Green. I'm not one of
those people who can remember every tiny event of
their childhood, but I can tell you that there was nobody at Camp Osceola called Pinky.

Still don't believe me? Then do this. Ask someone
who attended the second session of Camp Osceola in

1949 about this incident: After lunch one day, Skipper Macy — the director of the camp, and the man who always said "fine and dandy" — got on the subject of languages. Don't ask me why; I already told you that I don't remember every little detail. Skipper tried to find out which camper spoke the most languages — ordinarily, I'll admit, that was not a question that provoked intense competition at Osceola — and which camper do you think was finally called up on stage and slapped on the back by Skipper and told that it was fine and dandy? Right. Marc Rich. You have probably already guessed which Troop 61 Boy Scout — known up to that time mainly for his inability to do knots — said, "And to think . . . we're in the same tent." Right again. Me.

I hope you don't think I'm bringing this up to get a little reflected fame from the fact that my life-style was nurtured in the same tent as the life-style of the defendant in the single largest tax evasion case in the history of the republic — like those people in Kansas City who say they bought a necktie at Harry Truman's haberdashery on Thirty-first and Main. If everyone who says he bought a necktie from Harry Truman really had bought one, the store wouldn't have gone broke, and Harry Truman wouldn't have gone to the Senate, and Roosevelt would have been succeeded by William O. Douglas, and Clifton Daniels would be married to the daughter of a man who was known as "The Cravat King of K.C."

Marc Rich and I at Camp Osceola

The reason I'm telling you this is that the public should hear about Marc Rich from someone who actually knew him — instead of from all of those people who told the *Kansas City Times* that they couldn't quite remember which one he was. We were at Camp Osceola together, in the same tent. We actually sang the same song together at campfires. The song went like this:

> Softly falls the light of day,
> As our campfire fades away.
> Silently, each scout should ask,
> "Have I done my daily task?
> Have I kept my honor bright?
> Can I guiltless rest tonight?
> Have I done and have I dared
> Everything to be prepared?"

Now do you believe me?

I want you to know that what I am revealing about Marc Rich at Camp Osceola would be of no value to the FBI, which already knows that Marc speaks more languages than most Kansas City Boy Scouts and may even know that I can't do knots. I wouldn't rat on a pal. If I ratted on a pal, I couldn't guiltless rest tonight. I do think, though, that the public has a right to know about the Camp Osceola angle. I can just imagine the questions the reporters from the *Kansas City Times* — not to speak of the *New York Times* — would have asked me had they but known that Marc Rich and I

were in the same tent. They would want to know if
Marc and I — on campfire nights, as the fire was burning down to embers — talked about crude-oil prices
and arbitrage. They would want to know if Marc tried
to snooker any campers out of their canteen money.
They would want to know whether Marc was elected
to the Great Tribe of Mic-o-Say — whose song, sung
to the tune of "Oh Come All Ye Faithful," went "Oh
come all ye tribesmen, braves and mighty warriors,
oh come ye, oh come ye, to the Great Mic-o-Say" —
and if so, whether the Indian name he adopted (since
every tribesman adopted an Indian name) was something like He Who Buys Cheap and Sells Dear, or
maybe Brave Who Cooks the Books. They would want
to hear from someone who really knew Marc Rich.
That's why I'm revealing all of this.

to know during a long and eventful childhood in Kansas City, but I might just mention that Marc Rich has been charged with the single largest tax fraud in the history of the United States of America. I bring that up only as a way of demonstrating that we're not talking here about a column by someone who played kick-the-can with Bert Lance. We're talking about Marc Rich — the reclusive, elusive, fabulously wealthy commodities trader — and we're talking about the whole Camp Osceola angle. So why didn't anybody say "Wow!" or "Hey!" Why did they say things like "Uh-huh" or "I bet" or "Oh, sure"?

Why do people believe Ronald Reagan and not me? If Ronald Reagan said that the Communist headquarters they found in Grenada was the one they spent all that time looking for in Cambodia ten or twelve years ago, a lot of people would say: "Well, no wonder we couldn't find the damn thing the other time — we were looking in the wrong country. That must have been what the President meant when he said we got there just in time — in another few minutes they would have folded it up and moved it to Ecuador or maybe Wilkes-Barre." What would happen if Ronald Reagan — maybe while trying to distract public opinion from something embarrassing, like, say, destroying some small country by mistake — announced that he had gone to Boy Scout camp with Marc Rich? Do you think a lot of people would say "Uh-huh" or "I bet" or "Oh, sure"? A lot of people would say, "Hey! Wow! I used to think he was just some actor those rich right-wing nut cases got to front for them in California, but if he went to Boy Scout camp with Marc Rich . . . well, that's different."

I'd be furious, of course. I'd try to say something cool, like "Uh-huh," but sooner or later I'd start shouting, "He did *not* go to Boy Scout camp with Marc Rich! *I* went to Boy Scout camp with Marc Rich!" Ronald Reagan is twenty-four years older than Marc Rich, I would point out, once I had calmed down. So how could he have been at Camp Osceola at the same time?

"Well," one of the believers would say, "maybe he was held back."

"Held back! People don't get held back in Boy Scout camp! Held back? Held back twenty-four years in Boy Scout camp?"

"Well," the believer would say, "he *is* kind of slow."

Ronald Reagan doesn't know anything about Camp Osceola. Oh sure, he could sound as if he knew something about it if someone asked an Osceola question at a press conference. We've all read how he sucks up some facts from the briefing books like a giant turkey-baster and then squeezes them out over the Washington press corps (the same patsies, I just might point out, who failed to follow up the Nancy/Bubbles exposé). He *sounds* as if he knows something about Grenada, even though it couldn't have been very long ago that he thought Grenada was an MGM swashbuckler starring Cesar Romero. Reagan might be able to sound as if he knows about Camp Osceola — squeezing out a couple of little anecdotes about the Great

Tribe of Mic-o-Say, or Skipper Macy and the way he always used to say "fine and dandy" — but his knowledge of Osceola couldn't go deep. Mine goes deep.

For instance, if a reporter asked me whether Marc Rich ever cornered the market in any commodities at Osceola — and I'm really surprised that no reporter has asked that, although I suppose nothing should surprise me after their performance on the Nancy/Bubbles story — I would know that the only serious commodity at Camp Osceola was something called Chigger-Rid, which sometimes stopped the itching of chigger bites, although not usually.

Usually, nothing could stop the itching of a chigger bite short of amputation. Even though chiggers are exceedingly small compared with the huge mosquitoes people from various parts of the country are always bragging about — so small no protective clothing can keep them out, so small they cannot be spotted by the human eye — the itch of a chigger bite is just short of eternal. Growing up with chiggers changes your whole perspective on life. Sometimes, when I read about some Russian who was sent to a dreadful Siberian labor camp for whispering to his brother-in-law (who wanted his apartment) that the secret anti-Soviet provocateur headquarters the Red Army was looking for in Hungary wasn't in Afghanistan either, I say, "Well, at least it's too cold there for chiggers."

I know a lot of people who aren't from the Midwest aren't going to believe what I say about chiggers — about what a threat they are to our society and about how I'd rather invade St. Kitts single-handedly than walk through a vacant lot that might be harboring just one of them. For a long time, my own wife (an Easterner) thought I had made up chiggers. Made them up! Just because chiggers are so small you can't see them, they sometimes sound like a made-up bug, in the same way that Ronald Reagan sometimes sounds like a real-life President. Chiggers are real bugs. Is it my fault they don't have access to briefing books? You don't believe me? Ask Marc Rich. He was there.

Navasky as Felon

December 10, 1983

Now THAT the United States Court of Appeals has ruled that it was O.K. for the editor of *The Nation*, one Victor S. Navasky, to filch a manuscript of Gerald Ford's memoirs and spill the beans about the Nixon pardon, it has fallen upon me to explain the case to the layman. Fortunately, I am ideally suited for the task. I have kept abreast of the case from the start — except, of course, for the heist itself, which was solely the work of the aforementioned Navasky. It was I who had suggested that the book be titled *White House Memories of a Lucky Klutz*, or *Is This the Fairway for the Eighth Hole, or What?* It was I who pointed out that in an era when an unfairly dismissed busboy wouldn't think of suing for less than a million, suing Navasky for $12,500, the price of a publisher's lunch, might have been an attempt to make him out to be not just a thief but a small-time thief. Later, when Navasky slid back into a life of crime by lifting the manuscript of a book by Richard M. Nixon — an episode I have dealt with in detail in a study called "The Case of the Purloined Turkey" — it was I who urged him to seek help in rehabilitating himself, pointing out that the reporter who steals manuscripts of our political leaders' memoirs bears the burden of reading them. Now that I think of it, I'm surprised I wasn't called upon to testify at the Ford memoirs trial. I know plenty.

Here's what happened: Gerald Ford decides to write his memoirs, after getting an opinion from the White House counsel that the intent of those who framed the Constitution was that the President's salary include first serial rights and a fifty-fifty split on the paperback. (It is true that Jefferson got sixty-forty, but his agents were able to argue that he had published previous books, all of which earned back their advance.) Ford hires a ghostwriter, who would later testify that Ford was "not very anecdotal" — which is a nice ghostwriterly way of saying that he's the sort of man who isn't quite up to remembering what he had for breakfast. Ford's agent sells the book to Harper & Row and *Reader's Digest*, and that partnership in turn sells the constitutionally protected first serial rights to *Time*. So far, everybody is happy — except the ghostwriter, whose first six hours with Ford are spent coaxing out something like, "Bacon and eggs, I think, although that might have been yesterday."

Enter Sticky Fingers Navasky — through an open window, I suppose, unless he marched right past the receptionist, disguised as a lunchtime delivery boy bringing takeout to the publishers from Lutèce or the Four Seasons. (As I have stated, I have no firsthand knowledge of the alleged felony.) He filches the manuscript and writes a piece for *The Nation* revealing that Ford's book did not even mention some of the theories going around about why he pardoned Nixon — the theory that he had traded the pardon for an introduction to the best real estate broker in Palm Springs, for instance, or the theory that he had Nixon mixed up with a man named Dixon who had been arrested for climbing the Statue of Liberty in order to call attention to the plight of handicapped pets. *Time* says that it is no longer interested in printing excerpts from the book — thereby acknowledging publicly for the first time that its readership is identical to that of *The Nation* — and the publishers, led by Harper & Row president Brooks Thomas, sue Navasky for the pathetic twelve-five. Naturally, the case draws a lot of interest: because it involves the President's first serial rights, constitutional issues are involved. So far so good.

The first trial was in federal district court in Manhattan. I suspected things might not be going well for *The Nation*'s side when I noticed that every time Navasky sat in the witness chair next to the judge's desk the judge edged his silver water pitcher just out of Sticky Fingers' reach. Sure enough, the judge handed down a decision that, stripped of its judicial language and boiled down to a form that the layman can understand, amounted to this: Navasky is not just a thief but a small-time thief.

Navasky as Felon

Naturally, *The Nation* appealed. If you had a free lawyer, you'd appeal too. At the appeals court, *The Nation*'s free lawyer argued that in all of Navasky's article there were only 229 words of Ford's book that were under copyright, and even those weren't terribly interesting. The lawyer for *Reader's Digest* had a stronger case than the lawyer for Harper & Row: when the editors at *Reader's Digest* got through condensing Ford's book, 229 words were about all they'd end up using. For some reason, *The Nation*'s free lawyer concentrated on the First Amendment issue to the point of excluding what I had urged upon him as Navasky's two strongest arguments: (1) Since nothing is basically what Navasky pays all contributors to *The Nation*, not stealing Ford's memoirs would have left *The Nation* vulnerable to suits from other contributors under the equal protection provisions of the Fourteenth Amendment, and (2) There is a public health issue involved, since even the thought of paying for writing causes Navasky to break out in hives.

Even without those arguments, the Court of Appeals held for *The Nation*, with the majority decision being written by Judge Irving R. Kaufman — the same judge, it was widely noted, who presided over the trial of Julius and Ethel Rosenberg. Naturally, Navasky professed to be delighted with the decision, although it is my understanding that he was sort of hoping Judge Kaufman would give Brooks Thomas the chair — maybe just to scare him into revealing what he spends on those lunches. According to the *New York Times,* the case was important partly because it dealt with the distinction between facts, which cannot be copyrighted, and the "author's individual expression" — not an easy distinction to make, particularly when the expression of the author in question tends to be something like, "Maybe waffles; I like a waffle now and then, if they're not too done."

Bicycle Mishap

———

December 31, 1983

MY WIFE DESCRIBES my bicycle mishap as follows: "He fell off his bike." I would not describe it that way at all. Describing it that way makes it sound like the equivalent of some tenderfoot falling off his horse. That is not the way it was. A very large flatbed truck was involved, although in an indirect way. There is a sandy pavement to consider. All that is complicated, though, and rather technical. It's enough to say that the incident falls into the general category of bicycle mishaps and into the subcategory of bicycle mishaps in which the bicyclist in question lands on his face.

I didn't think of the implications of that subcategory until the next morning, when I went to the druggist for a supply of fresh bandages — looking, I must admit, like a middleweight who got what he deserved for climbing into the ring in such flabby condition.

"Animals!" the druggist said when I stepped up to the counter. "Vermin!"

I looked behind me. No animals. No vermin that I could see, although it is my impression that vermin are rather small, and might be hard to spot for someone whose glasses don't fit well over the bump next to his eye.

"They should put all the goddamned muggers in jail and throw away the keys!" the druggist said.

"I wasn't mugged," I said. "I was in a bicycle mishap."

"Whadidja — fall off your bike or something?" the druggist said.

"It wasn't that way at all," I said.

"Were you trying to get away from the muggers?" he said. "The bastards! They should send them all back to where they came from!"

"You see, there was this flatbed truck," I said. "One of those great, huge . . ."

But the druggist had turned away toward the cash register. He started ringing up my purchases. There was no indication that he was still thinking about my case, except that he occasionally muttered "Bastards!" or "Vermin!" as he punched the keys.

I have to say that I expected a little more concern from someone who would probably describe himself as being in a branch of the healing arts. There wasn't any doubt, after all, that I looked pretty gruesome: when I stopped at Joe's newsstand to get a paper, Joe took one look at my face and said, "Wow!"

"One of those great, huge flatbed trucks —"

"Did I ever tell you about the time I wrapped my

Pontiac GTO around the lamppost in front of the station house in Queens?" Joe said.

"I don't remember if you did, Joe," I said. "You see, my memory's not at its best because I was in this bicycle mishap, which started when this great, huge flatbed —"

"I guess I really had a load on," Joe continued, as if I hadn't spoken. "I climb out of the car, see, with blood streaming down my face, and all those cops are standing around me, 'cause they've rushed out of the station house when they heard the crash, and I point to the lamppost and say, 'The son of a bitch didn't even signal!' "

I tried to smile, although smiling really didn't do great things for some cuts I had around my mouth. I could still hear Joe chuckling as I walked away — past a couple of winos who sometimes sit on a park bench near Joe's newsstand. For the first time, they looked at me with sympathy instead of hostility.

"It happens to us all, brother," one of them said, shaking his head at the sadness of so many winos falling down drunk on hard pavements.

"It didn't happen to me, goddamn it!" I said. "I was in a bicycle mishap. There was this flatbed truck . . ."

The wino, though, seemed to have nodded off to sleep, and his companion was busy rummaging in a trash can next to the park bench.

It occurred to me that I might just stay home for a day or two. I didn't really want to spend my time hearing the details of other people's accidents or serving as an excuse for some diatribe on animals and vermin. I couldn't face going to the office and running into Harold the Committed — the fellow who is always asking me if I want to see civilization as we know it annihilated by a nuclear holocaust, even though I keep assuring him that I don't want to see civilization as we know it annihilated by a nuclear holocaust and at one point even offered to provide an affidavit to that effect. I would never be able to shake what would undoubtedly be Harold's first response to the sight of my lacerations — he would be convinced that I had finally gone to a demonstration against missile deployment, only to be brutalized by the hired thugs of the military-industrial complex — and I knew that after all these years I just couldn't handle Harold the Committed's all-out approval.

"Bicycle mishap," I said, in answer to the quizzical look I got from my neighbor McDougald, who was just leaving for work as I approached my house.

"One of 'em clipped you, huh?" McDougald said. "Bastards! Vermin! They ought to ban 'em!" He hurried down the street, trailing snatches of muttered complaints — ". . . no attention to red lights . . ." was one I heard, and ". . . zip the wrong way down . . ."

"No, there was this truck," I said, toward his back.

"What truck?" I heard someone behind me say. Mc-Dougald's wife had come out of the house just behind him, and she sounded genuinely interested. I told her about the truck.

"But weren't you following too close, then?" she asked. "And didn't you see the sand?"

"It is not customary to cross-examine the wounded," I said, proceeding to walk in a dignified way toward my door.

Howie the postman was just emerging. "What happened to you?" he asked.

I thought about it for a moment. Finally I said, "I fell off my bike."

The Buck Stops Over There

February 4, 1984

"DADDY, I DON'T UNDERSTAND why President Reagan took responsibility for the Marine Corps barracks in Beirut being bombed. He didn't do it, did he?"

"Of course not. He simply wanted to take credit for taking the blame. How about, as an extra treat this morning, some cereal that contains no riboflavin at all?"

"I think I like riboflavin, Daddy. Do you mean he gets credit for taking the blame the way George Washington got credit for admitting that he was to blame for chopping down the cherry tree?"

"Oh, no. Because George Washington really did chop down the cherry tree. You do get some credit for admitting something wrong you really did, but then everyone would know you did it. It's much better to take the blame for something you had nothing to do with. Everybody knows that Ronald Reagan wasn't in charge of making sure the perimeter of the Marine barracks in Beirut was secure. He lives in Washington, and doesn't work evenings."

"But you always taught me that if I've done something wrong, I'm supposed to tell the truth and admit it."

"Absolutely. Unless you go into politics. If a cherry tree in the White House Rose Garden got chopped down and all the evidence pointed to Ronald Reagan, he would say, 'I cannot tell a lie: there's a lady in California who picks up her welfare check every week in a Cadillac.' Would you like some more cereal? I read in the newspaper that there are no hungry children in America at all, and I wouldn't want to be responsible for spoiling the record."

"Do you mean you wouldn't really want to be responsible, or you wouldn't want to take the blame for being responsible, or you would want to take the credit for taking the blame?"

"Eat your cereal. You'll be late for school."

"But what if Ronald Reagan didn't chop down the cherry tree in the Rose Garden?"

"He did. He chopped it down."

"Really, Daddy. What if some White House gardener chopped down the tree by mistake?"

"Well, then, Reagan would take the blame, of course, because he obviously didn't have anything to do with it. He'd say that it was his responsibility because he was the head of the government that the gardener worked for. He'd say he still had a lot of faith in the gardener and that the gardener shouldn't be blamed.

And everybody would say that it was very decent of the President to take the blame for chopping down the cherry tree when it was obvious that he was absolutely blameless. They'd say that any man who can take the rap for his gardener is really a decent guy — a guy who probably has a lot of personal sympathy for poor people, if only they'd trade in their Cadillacs for some sort of compact. And the gardener would keep cutting down cherry trees until there weren't any more cherry trees."

"Daddy?"

"Yes?"

"Aren't you burning the toast?"

"It wasn't my fault. The sun was in my eyes. The ball hit a pebble."

"Daddy, weren't the people who got blamed for organizing the death squads in El Salvador really the people who did it?"

"I suppose so."

"And what happened to them?"

"They were sent into what the newscaster on the radio called 'diplomatic exile.'"

"What does that mean?"

"It means that they have to go someplace like France on an expense account."

"That's a punishment?"

"Why do you think I've always taught you that if you've done something wrong you're supposed to tell the truth and admit it? If you admit it to the right person, you might be sent to France on an expense account."

The Buck Stops Over There

"Did that man Charles Z. Wick who was secretly taping his phone conversations admit that he did it?"

"No, he denied that he did it — until the *New York Times* printed the evidence. That's another reason I've always taught you that if you've done something wrong you're supposed to tell the truth and admit it: you can never tell who might have a transcript."

"So did he get punished?"

"Not yet, but if the White House gets a lot of pressure from Congress and the press, he might have to go to France on an expense account, too. Would you like an egg this morning? I'm afraid somebody has ruined the toast. Probably the gardener."

"No, thank you. One thing I just thought of, Daddy: if the President takes the blame for something everyone knows he didn't do, then the person who was really to blame doesn't get blamed and neither does the President. So where does the blame go?"

"Would you like some more cereal?"

"Who was supposed to make sure the perimeter of the Marine barracks in Beirut was secure?"

"The Marine officers in charge."

"Well, why didn't they?"

"Well, partly because the Marines were sent there as a peacekeeping force and then they really became combatants but they were still trying to act like a peacekeeping force so it wouldn't have to be admitted that they were combatants."

"Who sent them there as a peacekeeping force?"

"Ronald Reagan."

"Who didn't want to admit that they had become combatants?"

"Ronald Reagan."

"Well, then, maybe he should have taken responsibility for the barracks being bombed because it was really his fault."

"I think I'll have a bowl of cereal myself, with riboflavin."

Alice as Tamperer

February 18, 1984

I WOULD LIKE to get on the record with my side of
the scale-tampering episode. Tampering occurred —
make no mistake about that. Any doubts anybody
might have had on that score were certainly put to
rest by the weighing of the Kitty Litter. But I'm getting ahead of the story. At the beginning, the object on
the scale was I, not the Kitty Litter. At the beginning,
it was I who shouted, "Somebody has been tampering
with this scale!"

I should state right now, in a straightforward manner, that my wife, Alice, was the leading suspect from
the start. That is not an easy thing to admit. Nobody
can be casual about acknowledging the possibility that
the woman he lives with — the mother of his children,
the daughter-in-law of his mother, the niece by marriage of his Uncle Benny — may be a scale tamperer.
Naturally, I considered every conceivable alternative
explanation. That did not take long. My daughters lack

a motive. They are, after all, too old to engage in some schoolyard boasting along the lines of "My daddy is fatter than your daddy." A sincere effort to think of people who might have slipped into our house for the purpose of tampering with the scale did not bear fruit. Is it really likely that some particularly competitive high hurdler fiddled with my scale to discourage me from competing in the Olympic trials? I don't think so. Is it possible that this was some bizarre retaliation for the questions I have raised now and then about the accuracy of the scales used by the proprietor of our local delicatessen, Lead Thumb Lindermann? I think not — although I'll admit that Lindermann would do almost anything that might provide him with a dramatic riposte ("I'll thank you to look to your own scales, sir!").

I have said that my daughters lack a motive. Can the same be said of Alice? If the scale had been adjusted downward, perhaps. The scale was not adjusted downward. In my experience, the scale is never adjusted downward. When scales start getting adjusted downward, some of the mistakes Lindermann absentmindedly makes in giving change will be in my favor. The tampering with my scale was an adjustment upward. For that, Alice has a motive.

Alice happens to have an intense — I am tempted to say obsessive — interest in my weight. I have assured her any number of times that she need not concern herself with this matter. I happen to have an excellent method of weight control myself: for thirty years now, I have dreamed of getting under the middle-weight limit and thus being the last man to fight Sugar Ray Robinson before his retirement. That is not quite true; my fantasy does not extend to the actual fight. What I picture is the weigh-in. Sugar Ray is looking confident as I step toward the scale. The scuttlebutt — probably traceable to Alice — is that I'll never make the weight. Sugar Ray's handlers are snickering and making snotty little remarks about my midsection ("I thought he was going to check that extra baggage, but I guess he intends to carry it aboard"). Sugar Ray him-self — ever the gentleman — tries unsuccessfully to suppress a grin as I step on the scale. The big arrow shoots up and then quivers to a stop: 159½. Sugar Ray's grin evaporates. A look of terror comes across his face.

"Did you say he was a middleweight or a light heavyweight?" Alice once said to me.

"Well, actually, he held the welterweight title until 1950, and then —" I stopped, suddenly aware that the question was not sincere. It cannot be easy to acknowl-edge that your wife is carrying on a campaign that includes sarcastic questions, but in order to get to the bottom of this entire sorry episode, such an acknowl-edgment must be made. I don't think that this is the place to explain in detail the campaign Alice carries on to control my weight. It is complicated and subtle and a bit distasteful. If I had to sum it up in a word, though, the word I would use is "nagging." Occasionally, as a change of pace, she uses sarcasm or ridicule — as in the aforementioned example. Until now, though, she has never resorted to scale tampering.

Which brings us to the deed itself. It took place on a sunny winter morning — one of those mornings that inspire confidence. I happened to take it into my head to weigh myself; I do that every year or so, just to keep up with things. It was then that I shouted, "Somebody has been tampering with this scale!"

Alice looked innocent. Alice can look fearsomely innocent when provoked. "Scale?" she said.

It was at that point that I decided to subject the scale to rigorous scientific tests. I looked around for a suitable test mechanism — a certifiably weighed object that I could weigh. My eyes fell on an unopened bag of Kitty Litter. Carefully I carried it to the scale — leaving the scale in precisely the same place, just in case position on the floor was what scientists call one of the variables. The bag of Kitty Litter was, according to the label, a ten-pound bag. On our scale, it weighed thirteen and a half pounds.

"The scale is set three and a half pounds too heavy," I said to Alice.

Alice thought for a moment. "It evens out at the higher weights," she said.

Evens out at the higher weights! This is science? The other way to look at it, I reminded Alice, is that the scale, in its tampered state, is approximately 33 percent too heavy, which means that an object shown to weigh 180 pounds may in fact weigh 120 — nearly forty pounds under the middleweight limit.

Alice, I am sorry to report, has not yet accepted that theory as completely proved. These days we often discuss such varying notions of mathematics — which is, of course, preferable to discussing my weight. "Have you weighed yourself lately?" Alice said the other day — changing the subject.

"No, I haven't," I said, "but I continue to weigh the Kitty Litter daily."

Disengagement

March 10, 1984

JUST WHEN I was beginning to think that no one else was interested in the question of the President's mental capacities, *Time* ran a piece in its February 6 issue on the growing evidence that Ronald Reagan is what it delicately called "disengaged." Oddly enough, "disengaged" was precisely the word *Newsweek* used a few years ago to describe the President — around the time he greeted Samuel Pierce, his Secretary of Housing and Urban Development, at a reception for mayors by saying, "How are you, Mr. Mayor? How are things in your city?" At the time, I confessed that I found the usage a bit cumbersome — it struck me as the equivalent of saying, "She's really more than a disengaged blonde" or "It was nothing but disengaged luck" — but apparently it has caught on in the news-magazine crowd.

Among the evidence *Time* presented to illustrate the President's disengagement was the fact that at a recent meeting with some governors he kept referring to EPA administrator William Ruckelshaus as Don — an eerie echo of the Samuel Pierce episode. According to *Time*, Reagan still isn't quite straight on which of his chief aides is in charge of what, and doesn't seem to know where their offices are; he is said to let his staff run the Executive Branch, staying out of their disagreements because he "lacks the temperament, and often the knowledge, to choose between the competing arguments." In speeches, *Time* said, Reagan sometimes buttresses his arguments with historical examples that turn out to be from movies, and in a meeting with a foreign leader last year he "pulled out and read from the wrong 4-in. by 6-in. cue cards." Disengaged move!

Time did not reveal the name of the foreign leader to whom Reagan read the wrong speech, but I like to think it was Margaret Thatcher. They are in the Oval Office, flanked by a few high-ranking diplomats. As Mrs. Thatcher finishes her remarks about how to deal with opposition to deployment of Pershing missiles in Western Europe ("A few strokes of the riding crop would sort out that lot"), Reagan takes some cards from his pocket. "My fellow Americans," he begins.

Mrs. Thatcher smiles politely, assuming that this is simply one more joke she doesn't get.

"I would like to tell you tonight the true story of one American who had a job to do and did it, and didn't join the crowd waiting around for a free ride from the government," the President continues.

"Quite right!" Mrs. Thatcher says. "A bunch of Bolshi layabouts!"

"It was in the American West, and this man came to a place where farmers and cattlemen were having some problems. His name was Shane . . ."

At about this point, as I envision it, the diplomats realize what has happened, and are, in *Time*'s phrase, aghast. They remain that way as Reagan continues with the story ("Come back, Shane . . .") or delivers a pitch about what the free enterprise system has enabled General Electric to produce for America. They are, as the saying goes, struck disengaged.

Being a magazine of some responsibility, *Time* made an effort to reassure those readers who might have become alarmed at the news that the President can't find his way around the White House. The story says that according to one White House aide, 80 percent of what Reagan doesn't know is unnecessary anyway. That kept me calm for a while, but then I began to wonder about the other 20 percent.

What I worry about is an emergency. I picture a slow afternoon in the White House — slow at least for the President. He is passing the time with a little exercise, working out cheerfully with a couple of ten-pound disengagedbells and trying to ignore the noise of Donald Regan and Martin Feldstein throwing chairs at each other in a nearby office. Suddenly, the hot-line telephone rings. It's Konstantin Chernenko. Reagan draws some cards from his pocket and tells Chernenko an inspiring story — the story of an American bar owner named Rick who didn't want to become involved in French politics in Casablanca but finally had to do what was right. But Chernenko has something else on his mind. He says American bombers seem to be approaching Soviet airspace, and if he doesn't get some reassurances from the White House right away, he is of a mind to let loose some missiles in the direction of Lawrence, Kansas.

However concerned I am about the 20 percent, I simply have to assume that the President knows for sure who Konstantin Chernenko is. It's been all over the papers. I'm just not up to entertaining the possibility that the President would respond to such a call by hanging up the phone, muttering "Some nut," and going back to his disengagedbells. I have to think he would dash into James Baker's office and ask what to do.

As we now realize, though, he doesn't know where James Baker's office is. What if he dashes into the office of, say, the White House caterer? The caterer is in his starched whites, and here the old identification problem reasserts itself: the President believes he is speaking to the Chief of Naval Operations.

"How are you, Admiral? How are things in the fleet?" Reagan says. "Oh, we had a call from Chernenko that you fellows'll probably want to look into first thing in the morning. Something about sending missiles to Kansas."

At that point, Donald Regan staggers into the room, bleeding slightly from a head wound Feldstein has managed to inflict with a Harvard Coop slide rule.

"How are you, George?" the President says, apparently mistaking Regan for former Senator George Murphy, an old Hollywood pal. "How are things in Glocca Morra?"

By that time, the caterer, a look of panic on his face, has opened the doors of the disengagedwaiter and climbed inside. In the Oval Office down the hall, the telephone has started ringing.

Beautiful Spot

March 31, 1984

READING THE ARTICLE *New York* ran on the multi-faceted life of Malcolm Forbes — who manages to publish a magazine and captain transcontinental balloon flights and amass great collections and oversee vast real estate holdings — I was interested mainly in his parking situation. We all have our own areas of specialty. Mine happens to be parking. I speak as the co-editor of *Beautiful Spot: A Magazine of Parking*, a pioneer publication in the parking media field. In fact, we are this very month celebrating the twenty-second anniversary of *Beautiful Spot*'s first issue — a celebration dampened in only the smallest way by the fact that the second issue has yet to appear.

It seems only yesterday that we were putting the first issue of *Beautiful Spot* to bed, but it was, as the diplomats say, many wars ago: the title of one piece was "The Algerian Problem (Parking in Algiers)." Time flies when you have production difficulties. My

co-editor, Gerald Jonas, was then in his heyday as perhaps the finest parallel parker on the West Side of
Manhattan — a multitalented man, in the Forbes mold,
who could back in well enough to be known as Two
Turns Jonas and could also unearth for our premiere
issue a moving poem on parking tickets (usually cred-
ited to the noted Brooklyn sonneteer L. M. Bensky):

> The smalla the space the smalla the fella
> Sez my cop, who puts the green things
> Happy and stringy like angels' bright wings
> On the cars nearest the thingamajig
> Which can't be parked within fifteen feet of.

Jonas and I no longer work steadily on *Beautiful
Spot*, but naturally I like to keep a hand in. That's why
a passage in the article on Malcolm Forbes caught my
eye: "He had begun his working day seated beside the
chauffeur-bodyguard in the leather seat of his bronze
Maserati, which is equipped with a telephone, New
York Press plates —" Stop right there! New York Press
plates? Although *Beautiful Spot* did not deal with New
York Press plates in its first issue, that subject was on
our list of future stories, along with "Parking and the
Jewish Question" and a polemic called "Let's Put the
Park Back in Park Avenue." I bring the list of future
stories up to date now and then, just in case our production difficulties clear up, and I have just put at the
top of the list a piece to be called "What Is Malcolm
Forbes Doing with New York Press Plates?"

Is it possible that he covers those fast-breaking stories that require a reporter to screech to a halt in front of a burning building and leap out of his car, with no time to search for a parking spot? I tried to picture the action in the *Forbes* newsroom as word of a fire in a Bronx chicken-feather warehouse comes over the police radio, and Forbes is assigned the story by the gruff city editor (also named Forbes). "Forbes!" Forbes shouts. "Get on your roller skates and get out to that two-alarmer in the Bronx. If that joint burns down, the chicken-feather market's going to go through the roof and we'll have a scoop. If Max Fortune of *Fortune* beats you out there, don't bother to come back."

I should say right here that "Get on your roller skates" is a figure of speech, peculiar to city editors. A man who has a bronze Maserati with a chauffeur-bodyguard does not roller-skate to the Bronx. But wouldn't covering a fire present special problems for someone with a three-million-dollar car? I can imagine some sooty spray falling dangerously near the Maserati as firemen desperately soak down the warehouse. The chauffeur-bodyguard instructs the fire department lieutenant in charge to redirect the hoses, using that turn of speech peculiar to chauffeur-bodyguards: "Watch the paint job, creep."

So, as we say in the trade, I made a few calls. I asked a few questions. Why, for instance, are the stretches of curb reserved by "NYP Plates Only" signs so far from police headquarters and so convenient to the theater district? Do newspaper editors who leave their cars in Larchmont during business hours really need NYP spaces near midtown restaurants, where they like to spend long evenings congratulating one another on exposés of Congressmen who pull rank to bump decent folks off airplanes? It must be clear by now that the delay of *Beautiful Spot*'s second issue has not been caused by any lack of aggressive, hardnosed reporting. We've had production difficulties.

Here is what I uncovered: The State Department of Motor Vehicles, which has nothing at all to do with the "NYP Plates Only" signs, certifies certain organizations as news-gathering organizations but leaves it to them to provide the names of those employees in need of NYP plates. (If the person who provides the list would rather include a police reporter in Queens than the man who pays his salary, fine.) The Bureau of Traffic Operations puts up the "NYP Plates Only" signs but has nothing to do with assigning the plates that make it possible to park in front of them. In other words, if you can find out precisely who is responsible for giving magazine publishers special parking privileges in New York, you can probably find out precisely who was responsible for involving this country in the Vietnam War — a war, I regret to say, which production difficulties caused *Beautiful Spot* to miss completely, much to the disappointment of readers who were looking forward to an article we had promised on the exotic parking meters of Hue.

Beautiful Spot

Here is what worries me: When other influential people in New York realize that NYP plates have virtually nothing to do with gathering the news, they'll want special plates of their own. The garment industry will demand NYSB plates for designated shmata barons, and that will bring a demand for NYRES plates from the real estate sharks. The average parker — *Beautiful Spot*'s loyal reader — will see all of these special plate signs going up as he circles the block again and again, looking for a spot. Malcolm Forbes will have nothing to worry about: he'll have his New York Big-Time Collector plates and his New York Transcontinental Ballooner plates, among others. *Beautiful Spot* will do an article on his multifaceted parking life, as soon as our production difficulties are cleared up.

Nuclear War:
My Position

April 21, 1984

LOOKING FOR WAYS to ease my mind about signs that the danger of nuclear war is increasing, I stumbled across one comforting thought: maybe the Russian missiles won't work. I realize that the possibility of a simple malfunction is a thin reed upon which to hang the survival of the species. Still, it's what I have for now, and I'm going with it. I have adopted it as my new. official position on the entire nuclear arms issue. It may sound like a fallback position, but as it happens, I have already fallen back. Before I adopted my new position on the issue of nuclear arms I had a rather complicated position which, stated in its simplest terms, was as follows: "I'd rather not think about it."

I owe my new position to a passage I read in an interesting piece on the arms race by Thomas Powers in *The Atlantic* a couple of months ago. "Don't judge Russian missiles by your TV set," Powers was told in Mos-

cow after he happened to mention to one of the people
he was interviewing that the television set in his hotel
room didn't work. "Some things we *can* do." Powers
can believe that if he wants to. I'd rather not. I prefer
to believe that the Russian missiles won't work because their television sets don't work.

Why didn't I think of this years ago? I have certainly
read enough about the shoddiness of goods produced
by Soviet industry — overcoats whose sleeves fall off
now and then, television sets permanently tuned to the
all-snow channel, refrigerators destined to become the
only thing in a Moscow apartment that is never cold. I
have read about those Russian tractor factories where
vodka-sodden workers fulfill their monthly quota in a
frantic last-minute push that can succeed only if they
attach the transmissions with Scotch tape. Why have
I always taken it for granted that those goofballs would
be so good at annihilating continents?

Naturally, my new official position came equipped
with what the nuclear strategists call a scenario. It
went like this: When the nuclear exchange finally
comes, all the Russian missiles fizzle on their launch-
ing pads except one, which destroys Punta del Este,
Uruguay. Our missiles destroy Russia. The second
part of the scenario was based on easily obtainable and
incontrovertible data concerning the operating efficiency of television sets in American hotel rooms. Television sets in American hotel rooms work. Considering
what's shown on them, you might argue that they
work to a fault — but they work.

When I first adopted my new official position, I was often asked if I felt guilty that the Russians would be destroyed in a nuclear exchange while we survived without a scratch, and I often answered, "Not as guilty as you might think." After all, I never claimed that this was anything but a fallback position. Also, I was relieved to have some progress to report to the fellow we call Harold the Committed, who is constantly asking me if I really want to see civilization as we know it destroyed in a nuclear holocaust.

"I think I've got some good news on that front, Hal the C," I said, the next time he asked. "Apparently Tom Powers could only get the snow channel in Moscow, plus one channel where the vertical was totally out of whack."

Harold the Committed seemed unable to make the connection, but I was certain that the implications of the video efficiency gap would not be lost on a Russian counterpart of Thomas Powers — a journalist named, say, Raskolnikov, who comes to America to do interviews for a piece on nuclear arms. Switching on the television set in his Washington hotel room in the hope of seeing some snow that might bring back memories of his boyhood in the heroic Siberian settlement of Yakutsk Molymsk, he is astonished to find an absolutely clear picture on sixteen channels. He is glued to the set. He watches two morning news programs. He watches *Donahue*. He watches *Sesame Street*. He watches *Gilligan's Island* reruns. He watches the soaps. Late in the afternoon, as he is watching a closed-

circuit hotel channel on shopping opportunities in Alex-
andria, the telephone rings. It's the Pentagon general
Raskolnikov was supposed to interview six hours
earlier. Raskolnikov rushes to the Pentagon, bursting
with stories of the magic box in his hotel room.

"They work like a charm, Mr. Raskolnikov," the general says. "Out at the house, I have my twenty-six-
incher hooked up to one of those satellite dishes, and
get a hundred and twenty-eight channels, clear as a
bell. I get restless at four in the morning, I watch the
rugby from Melbourne. I'm glad you noticed how well
that little mother works."

"What I noticed," Raskolnikov says, "is that it was
made in Japan."

Well, yes, there's that. The television sets that work
so well are made in Japan. The general in the Pentagon cautions Raskolnikov against judging America's
technological capabilities by the fact that our television
sets have to be imported from Japan. He tells Raskolnikov that through state-of-the-art technology and a
finely meshed military chain of command, we could
annihilate Russia with the flick of a switch. Raskolnikov can believe it if he wants to. Can any American
who has ever served in the Army or owned a car made
in Detroit believe it? I'd rather not believe it. Who
wants to feel even a little guilty about destroying Russia while it's only knocking off Punta del Este?

On that day of days, according to my revised scenario, the politicians order the missiles fired at the
enemy, but then nothing much happens. The Russian

commander raises his hand to give the signal, and the left arm of his overcoat falls off; during the delay, tractor transmissions drop out of the missiles. Our guys are missing two D-size batteries necessary for flicking the switch that activates our finely meshed chain of command, and the second lieutenant authorized to procure replacements is off waxing his GTO. In a couple of hours, it's all over. That is, it's all over but it's not *all over*. The Russians get a stiff note from Uruguay. Otherwise, the world is as it was. It will remain that way, according to my analysis, until one side or the other gets a Japanese-made missile.

of mine, of course, but I just thought I'd mention it — as long as the subject happened to come up. I think I have the credentials to make such a judgment as the author of *The Jet Lagger's Guide to What's Doing in Portland at Four-Thirty in the Morning* and a tone poem called "Asleep at Lunch in Tacoma — Alas, Oh Woe." I don't suppose the White House people have ever read what I've written on jet lag. Fine. Nobody's forcing them. Maybe they were bedazzled by the credentials of the man they chose as the chief jet-lag briefer, Charles Ehret, a biologist at the Argonne National Laboratory. Maybe they had their people look into my scientific background (Geology 101), and some snoop came up with my grade for the semester. I'm not going to argue about any of that. Just for the record, though, Ehret's all wrong. Also just for the record, there were mitigating circumstances in Geology 101.

I heard about the jet-lag briefing on the radio, but those of us in the field have been familiar with Ehret's theories for some time. Ehret says that by alternating days of feasting and fasting in the week before you leave — and completely abstaining from anything alcoholic — you can adjust your body clock to the new time. What that really amounts to is this: starving and stuffing yourself on alternate days, without even an occasional belt to smooth out the switches, makes you feel so miserable that even flying sixteen hours across eight or ten time zones is an improvement. Saying that you feel better at your destination after following Ehret's regimen is like saying that you feel better as a civilian after a couple of years in the Army. How does Ehret's theory explain the experience of a reporter I know who claims to avoid any effect of transcontinental jet lag by a method he describes as "drinking so much on the plane that I don't know what day it is"? How does Ehret explain the fact that even though I left Kansas City for good in 1953 my body clock remains on Central Standard Time? I don't mean to criticize. It's really none of my concern.

I might not have had time to brief the President anyway. I've been very busy. As a citizen, I'm usually happy to pitch in, but I really can't say that I would definitely have been able to find time to brief the President on one of my specialties — jet lag, say, or the Quemoy and Matsu issue. Someone who happens to be a specialist on at least two subjects can't be expected to drop everything, pick up his briefing books, and dash off to Washington every time a President decides to go to China. It's of no great importance to me, of course, but I'd be kind of curious to know who they finally got to do the Quemoy and Matsu briefing. As far as I know, I'm the only person who has mentioned Quemoy and Matsu in print in the past ten or twelve years, so it's not as if Quemoy and Matsu specialists are thick on the ground.

Maybe they didn't get anyone. After all, if someone had explained to the President that a major issue in the 1960 presidential campaign was whether it was worth going to war to prevent China from taking over the offshore islands of Quemoy and Matsu, he might also have had to explain why the prospect of being taken over by China was considered so horrifying. And that would require bringing up a subject the White House aides must have wanted to avoid: China is in the hands of the Communists. If the President had been reminded of that, he wouldn't have made the trip — he doesn't like Communists — and his aides wouldn't have had a crack at the moo shu pork. They would probably claim that telling him about China's being Communist would fall within the category of details they don't like to burden him with, lest he, like Jimmy Carter, become so obsessed with minutiae that he begins arranging the schedule for use of the White House tennis court. In fact, there is no danger at all of this President becoming ensnarled in tennis court scheduling: he can't remember the players' names.

If the President was briefed on Quemoy and Matsu, it must have been by a briefer who was willing to concoct some reason other than Communism to explain our concern in 1960. Some people would do that sort of thing, I suppose, just for a chance to do a presidential briefing. Why should the rest of us specialists criticize such people just because we still have our integrity?

What could have happened from that sort of briefing is obvious. There is the President having dinner in the private quarters of Deng Xiaoping, and Deng brings up the question of Quemoy and Matsu.

"Well, sorry we had to be on the other side on that one back then," the President says. "I know you fellows wanted those islands, but, as you know, Brazil also had a claim, and we really needed that coffee for our steel mills."

Deng gives the President a puzzled look, but the President has fallen asleep into his moo shu pork.

There has been nothing in the press coverage suggesting such an incident, but I wonder if we have really been told everything that happened over there. I'm certainly not saying that it would serve the White House right if the President was embarrassed on account of his briefing. I just thought I'd mention it.

Low Visibility

June 2, 1984

I HAVEN'T SEEN any of the mountains I was meant to see. That doesn't sound right. That sounds like somebody saying, "Alas! I was born to see mountains, yet I have spent my entire life within the environs of Ottumwa, Iowa." That is not what I mean. I mean that I have been in places where you're supposed to see certain mountains, and I have not been able to see them. When I am in parts of France where the Alps are visible on a clear day, for instance, it is not a clear day. In Japan, I did not see Mount Fuji. I missed Mount McKinley in Alaska. From a splendid perch on the top row of an ancient amphitheater in Taormina, Sicily, I failed to see Mount Etna in the distance. In Tanzania, I was unable to make out Mount Kilimanjaro. There might have been snows on Kilimanjaro and there might not have been snows on Kilimanjaro. For all I know, Gregory Peck and Ava Gardner were still up there. I couldn't see a thing.

There is no question that in each case I was in a spot from which the mountain is, in theory, viewable. When I realized that I was not going to see Mount Rainier, in fact, I was standing on the porch of the Mountain View Inn. Also, I would like to dispose at once of the notion that I might have actually seen the mountains in question and not recognized them as mountains. I know where that kind of talk comes from. It comes from people who know that I have never been able to see constellations. It is true that every time someone has said to me, "There — can't you see Orion's belt, starting with that bright star over on the left?" I have said, "No, not really." I have never seen Orion or his belt. I'll admit that I wasn't looking very hard for a while, since I thought for years that Orion was O'Ryan, and I considered the possibility of an Irish constellation unlikely. Even after I knew Orion's name, though, I couldn't see him. I don't think the people who are always pointing him out to me can see him either. I think the constellation business is purely arbitrary. I think there are just a bunch of stars up there. I think that if you said to one of the constellation people (in a sufficiently authoritative tone), "Good view of Athena's dirndl tonight over there; you can even see where the hem's coming loose," he would nod sagely and say something about the natural wonders of the universe.

All of which leads me to turn the tables on this talk about whether I can recognize a mountain when I see one: it may be that the people who are always saying that they saw the mountains did not really see them.

People are like that. I was never sure that all the people who used to say that they found French movies
meaningful really found French movies so meaningful. I still feel that way about all the people who say
there is nothing in the world they would rather eat
than a fresh asparagus. I think it's possible that a lot
of people — the same sort of people who say they see
belts and pots and all sorts of knickknacks in the
sky — just look squinty-eyed through the fog toward
the mountain and say, "Hmmm. Yes. Lovely."

Maybe some of them don't like to admit that they
missed the mountain. Let's say that a man named
Thistlethwaite returns from the trip to Japan that he
has looked forward to for years, and his brother-in-
law — the boorish brother-in-law who's always saying
that Thistlethwaite paid too much for his car and went
to the wrong discount store for the grass-edger — says
that Mount Fuji must have been quite a sight, even for
someone who might well have been preoccupied with
having paid the straight coach fare to Tokyo when he
could have put together a charter-and-excursion pack-
age through Honolulu. Is Thistlethwaite really going
to say, "Actually, we didn't see Fuji, what with the low-
lying clouds"? Does he want to hear his brother-in-law
say, "Hey Marge — did you hear that? Did you hear
they dropped a bundle going over there to Japan and
missed the main mountain?"

I think not. I think Thistlethwaite is more likely to
shake his head in wonderment and say, "Yes, quite a
sight, quite a sight." What does he have to lose? He

isn't likely to be questioned closely on what the mountain looked like, and even if he is, it's the simplest thing in the world to fake: "Tall. It was tall. And pointy at the top. Tall and pointy."

I want to make this clear right now: I am not complaining. You won't find me grabbing people by the lapels at parties and saying, "Why is it that everybody gets to see the mountains but me?" For one thing, it is not true that everybody gets to see the mountains but me. My wife, for instance, doesn't get to see them. She is usually with me, standing in the fog. I'm not complaining and I'm not being defensive. There is nothing defensive about pointing out that all the inspirational stuff about mountains does not apply in this case. The nun in *The Sound of Music* keeps telling everyone to climb every mountain. Well, fine. But you can't climb them if you can't see them, Sister. Also, there is the matter of George Mallory, the great English mountain climber, who answered the question of why he wanted to climb Mount Everest by saying, "Because it's there." But what if he had been asked what he would do if the mountain was not, in fact, there? He'd have said, "Well, then, I wouldn't climb it, you silly twit! Is this your idea of a joke, or what?" So much for the inspirational stuff.

I don't want to hear any reassurances that it's not my fault. I know perfectly well that it's not my fault. How can someone blame himself for low-lying clouds? The reassurances remind me of the way people used to talk about Jimmy Carter: "Well, of course, it wasn't

his fault that he was in office when the Iranians decided to take over the American Embassy — but,
still . . ." Carter's mistake, I keep reading, was in not
emphasizing the positive. The mountains I have not
seen are renowned mountains, after all. They are high
mountains. I have missed seeing a total of nearly one
hundred thousand feet of exceedingly renowned mountains. That is not counting the Alps. I haven't decided
yet whether I should count all the Alps or just the ones
I specifically couldn't see. I'm leaning toward counting all of them.

I Say!

June 23, 1984

ACCORDING TO the *New York Times,* a survey taken
recently in Western Europe indicates that Europeans
don't much like the English. No news there. The organization responsible for the survey — the European
Economic Community — says that the hostility toward
Great Britain is the result of a dispute now going on
over the EEC's spending practices and agricultural
program, but I don't think that's it at all. I think that
Europeans are hostile toward the English because the
English have some irritating habits — the habit, for
instance, of ending sentences with questions that
sound like reprimands. You say it's difficult for you to
tell because you haven't read the survey? Well, you'll
have to read it then, won't you. See how snotty that
sounds? It sounds as if the person who said it expects
you to say, "Well, yes, I suppose I will have to read it,
and it was terribly stupid of me not to have realized
that before." Think how snotty it would sound in an

English accent. Think how snotty it would sound to a Frenchman whose understanding of English may be imperfect and who might have thought that the Englishman was saying, "Quit standing on my foot — would you?" It sounds snotty, but the English actually don't mean anything by it. They don't know any other way to talk.

Why do the English talk so funny? For one thing, they're all hard of hearing. All Englishmen are hard of hearing. That's why they end a lot of sentences with questions — just to check and make sure the other fellow heard what they were saying. (When you think about it that way, it's not snotty; it's actually rather thoughtful.) That's why they're always saying "I say!" It gives the other fellow a warning that they're about to say something, and then he knows to tune in. This used to be a secret — that all Englishmen are hard of hearing. All the English knew, of course, but they wouldn't let it out to foreigners. I'm the one who found out about it. I found out watching Harold Pinter plays.

The people in Harold Pinter plays are very hard of hearing. That is what professors of drama mean, I suppose, when they talk about how a dramatist has a heightened sense of reality: he takes people who are just hard of hearing and he makes them very hard of hearing. People in Pinter plays are always repeating themselves because the other character didn't hear them the first time:

"Hello."

"What?"

I Say!

"Hello."

"I thought you said good-bye."

"No. Hello."

"What?"

"Good-bye."

Even after I uncovered the secret of Harold Pinter,
I tried to keep it to myself. I had learned my lesson
several years before, when I revealed that the Italian
movies everybody considered so profound would seem
silly to anyone who understood Italian. I wasn't claim-
ing that I understood Italian; in fact, Italian often
sounds to me as if the speaker is telling a lot of other
people to quit standing on his foot. I was just saying
that Americans who went to see an Italian movie that
had been called profound concentrated hard on getting
the subtitles read before the scene changed, figured
that a lot of nuances must have been lost in reducing
great hunks of dialogue into one line of type, and
didn't stop to consider the possibility that the movie
was simply silly. Then a couple of the profound Italian
directors made their first movies in English, and all
the critics said the movies were silly. I thought the
critics would then realize that all the movies they had
said were profound would also have seemed silly if only
they had understood the dialogue, but instead they said
that even a profound director can't hit every time at
bat. I also thought a lot of people would come up to
me and apologize for having called me a philistine and
a hopeless lout, but nobody did. So when people asked
what I thought of Harold Pinter plays — even after I

knew the secret — I just said, "Very English. His plays are very English."

Of course, the dispute at the headquarters of the European Economic Community must have been exacerbated by the special way that people who go into the British diplomatic service talk — particularly their habit of putting together packages of adverbs and adjectives that don't match, like "perfectly awful" and "frightfully nice." I know they don't mean anything by it, but it can't be much fun to listen to all the time. The French representative to the EEC must get the feeling that he's constantly being served a chocolate parfait with béarnaise sauce.

"I say!" the representative of the United Kingdom says, although the warning is quite unnecessary, since the French hear better than anyone (that's why they talk so fast).

"Please don't," the French representative says. "At least not so soon before lunch."

At this point, I assume, the Italian representative has the wit to speak only in subtitles.

It can't help that what the English want to discuss in the EEC is the agricultural program. While the French or Belgian or Italian representative is politely negotiating an agreement for exporting vegetables to the United Kingdom, he is secretly seething with the knowledge that the English are going to overcook them. This must be the sort of thing diplomats are referring to when they talk about hidden agendas. The French representative is supposedly talking in purely economic terms about the exportation of asparagus, but the memory of what the British had done to a French asparagus he once encountered in Brighton is causing him to negotiate through clenched teeth. The British representative sails along without noticing.

"I say! That would be terribly good," he says, as the agreement is reached.

"But is it the green asparagus or the white asparagus that you want, monsieur?" the French representative says.

"Well, that's up to you," the Englishman says. "Isn't it."

Loony

I RAN INTO an academic friend of mine called Big
Grant Beckerman and found him looking distraught.
By now, of course, I'm accustomed to seeing Big Grant
in a nervous state: he applies for so many grants that
he's virtually always facing some sort of deadline.
"Can't stop to talk now," he'll say. "The Carnegie proposal's got to be in by four. I still owe the Rockefeller
panel three support letters on the history consultancy.
Also, if this budget narrative isn't Federal Expressed to
NIMH overnight tonight we're out of the running.
Good to see you." That final remark is usually barely
audible, since Big Grant is already scurrying down the
street, half trotting while pawing through a bulging
briefcase for the forms he's always worried about losing. On those rare days when Big Grant isn't facing a
deadline he is likely to be upset by one of the rumors
he's heard about the grant-giving world — some horrifying tale about how some government agency might

be planning to change its emphasis from replication to felt need.

This time, though, Big Grant seemed disconsolate rather than anxious. "What's the matter, Big?" I asked. "You look as if you've just heard that the Ford Foundation decided to give all the money back to Henry."

"NEH," Big Grant said. "Haven't you heard?"

"NEH?"

"The National Endowment for the Humanities," Big Grant said. "The Reagan Administration is packing the board with loonies."

I had, in fact, read that the Reagan Administration's recent nominations to the council overseeing NEH grants had been interpreted as indicating an intention to make the council a repository for what I believe intellectuals refer to as the Meshugeneh Right. Describing the new nominees, Richard Lyman, a former vice-chairman of the council who is president of the Rockefeller Foundation, told the *New York Times*, "The chief common thread seems to be working for the right-to-life movement." From other news accounts, I gathered that the principal intellectual credential of one nominee is the co-chairmanship of the Virginia chapter of the Moral Majority.

At the time, I rather enjoyed picturing a meeting of the NEH council once the Reagan folks had it completely packed with true believers. I saw it as a kind of nutso United Nations. The consideration of almost any proposal causes one of the council's Moral Majority preachers to rail against heathenism and enjoyable fornication. The other council members are having difficulty concentrating on the sermon, though, because a couple of former HUAC investigators (both of them emeritus professors of the history of subversion at Pepperdine) are crawling around under the boardroom table, looking for Communists. Somebody else is sniffing suspiciously at the water pitcher, on the lookout for a fluoridation plot. At the end of the table, an intense-looking man with a 1950s crew cut has buttonholed the council member next to him and launched what promises to be a four-hour explanation of why this country is a republic, not a democracy. The right-to-life people are noisily unrolling huge posters of fetuses. In the corner, a couple of Young Americans for Freedom huddle together, discussing socialist inroads and acne remedies. A lobbyist for the Heritage Foundation is standing on his chair to finish assembling a plaster-of-Paris model of the American Way of Life.

"For it is as in the final days of Rome," the preacher is saying. "Despoliation and unnatural acts and liquor by the drink . . ."

"Be sure to check the drawers," one of the ex-HUAC gumshoes is saying to his partner as they clonk around under the table. "Lots of times they hide in drawers, way in the back."

I should have realized that Big Grant Beckerman, a man accustomed to analyzing the members of grant panels the way a devout horse-handicapper studies the nags, could hardly be expected to find such unchartable chaos entertaining. I tried to cheer him up by reminding him that he had adapted to changing moods in Washington in the past. When the Carters were talking a lot about grassroots culture, Big Grant submitted a proposal for a traveling exhibit of books and manuscripts called "Home-Grown: A Display of the Local and Mediocre." When Reagan named a neoconservative to chair the NEH, Big Grant submitted a history proposal with a thesis that amounted to this: slavery was bad, of course, but could the slaves be said to have suffered compared to the Yeshiva student on Norman Podhoretz's block in Brooklyn who lived in constant peril of being ridiculed by black teen-agers for throwing like a girl?

"This is different," Big Grant said sadly. "This is the cuckoo club."

"Why not approach it head-on, Big?" I said. "An epic poem about the value of loonies in American life."

"I could never think of a rhyme for 'wackos,'" Big said. "Maybe I'll go back to teaching." He shuddered.

"Tobaccos," I said.

"Tobaccos?"

"A rhyme for wackos,'" I said.

Big Grant just shook his head. He looked beaten — a traveling salesman who has just lost his biggest account. I had to remind Big Grant that there was a problem with his going back to teaching. Several years ago, he confessed to me that he had forgotten his original academic discipline. I don't mean that he was rusty on the material; I mean he had forgotten what his original academic discipline was.

Big Grant considered that for a while. Finally he said, "I suppose it could begin, 'Ever since the settlers came here and found Indians curing various tobaccos / America has depended on its wackos.'"

"Well, something along that line," I said.

But Big Grant didn't seem to hear me. He was pawing through his briefcase. "I think the poetry deadline's this week," he said. "Got to get the forms. Can't stop to talk. Good to see you."

Baker Redux

—

September 1, 1984

EARLIER THIS SUMMER, Russell Baker, the distinguished columnist for the *New York Times*, reported
in his column that he had nearly been run down by an
unidentified, presumably homicidal bicyclist on the
streets of Manhattan. I am now prepared to say that
I was that bicyclist. There! I've said it! What a load off
my chest! I almost feel like confessing to a lot of
things I had nothing to do with. Not quite. I was not
responsible, for instance, for the plan to install Bert
Lance as chairman of the Democratic National Committee. I know some people have been saying otherwise. (That kind of talk gets back to a person.) In
1981, it is true, I confessed in public print that every
national administration made me nostalgic for the
previous one. I even revealed that I had been heard
to say, about the time the Reagan Administration was
beginning to get its nose in the trough, "Come back,
Bert Lance — all is forgiven." What I said about Bert

Lance, though, was meant as a little joke. It was obviously not a request for action. I've just admitted, right here in front of everybody, that I almost ran down a distinguished columnist on the streets of Manhattan, but I had nothing to do with the Bert Lance decision and I don't intend to take the rap for it.

I meant Russell Baker no harm. I like Baker. I did what I did for his own good. Believe me, what I did hurt me more than it hurt him — although if I had managed to hit him I suppose it would have hurt him more. In his column, he acknowledged that he had walked into the intersection without checking to see if any bicycles were coming the wrong way down a one-way street. In other words, there were things about the city Baker still didn't know. I was trying to teach him. I used the method boxing coaches use when they first get in the ring with a new welterweight. They say, "Now, lower your guard." The welterweight lowers his guard. They punch him in the nose. Then they say, "That'll teach you never to lower your guard." This is for the welterweight's own good. By actual measurement — Rutgers did a study on this — it hurts the welterweight more than it hurts the coach, but it's still for the welterweight's own good.

In his column, Baker admitted that he got some bad advice before moving to the city. People warned him about the danger of being shot and then stuffed into the trunk of a car, gangland style — something that has happened to him hardly at all — but they neglected to mention the danger of being mowed down by a bicycle. In fact, they neglected to mention something else: in New York, if the mob has any thoughts at all about rubbing you out gangland style, they warn you by having somebody run you down with a bicycle. This has replaced the old kiss-of-death business, which some of the younger mobsters decided was sort of sloppy and not that great for the mob's image. In other words, the close call I gave Baker was not simply a warning to keep an eye out for bicycles coming the wrong way down one-way streets. It was also a warning about what can happen to you in New York if you get the idea that it might be fun to borrow money at high interest from someone who is a lot bigger than you and wears a fedora. Nearly running somebody down with a bicycle is also a general warning, in the way a punch in the nose can be a general warning. As a general warning it means this: Never lower your guard.

Baker is not the only person I have helped in this way. Often, when I read that some distinguished citizen is moving to New York, I take it upon myself to come close to running him down on my bicycle. It's my version of the Welcome Wagon. If New York University has landed a world-class professor for its law school, for instance, I try to brush him back onto the curb some sunny afternoon as he strolls over to Washington Square to see if there are any interesting torts among the chess players. Like a lot of people who do good works, I try to be unobtrusive. I'm not one of those maniacal types you may have noticed bent over four-pound racing bikes — a wild look in the eyes and a whistle clamped between the teeth just in case there is a sudden need to terrify an aged pedestrian. I ride a blue Raleigh three-speed with an exceedingly large basket on it — the 1979 Plymouth station wagon of bicycles. Someone who saw me pedaling quietly up Sixth Avenue might take me for the senior delivery boy at Gristede's supermarket, never dreaming that I was on my way uptown to pay my respects, in a manner of speaking, to the new British ambassador to the United Nations.

Has anybody been hurt? That's what they're always asking the boxing coach: Well, that's all very well, coach, but did you ever break anybody's nose that way? Did you ever give anybody emotional asthma or maybe a snoring problem that proved a considerable liability to an otherwise stable marriage? No. Nobody has ever been hurt. Once, through the unforeseen and sudden appearance of a Sabrett's hot-dog cart, the new first violinist of the New York Philharmonic, a smallish man, was carried several hundred yards in my delivery-boy basket, but he didn't seem upset. In fact, he asked if I'd be interested in delivering him to rehearsals daily. I told him politely that I had some other tasks to do on my bike. Then I rode off alone into the sunset.

What is unusual about the Russell Baker incident, of course, is that Baker is not really a newcomer. It must be eight or ten years since he wrote a particularly memorable piece about the dangers facing anyone who moves to the city: Baker, unable to think of an idea

for a column, had gone for a short walk and was almost beaned by a potato that had fallen from a high-
rise. Ordinarily, I wouldn't bother to run down anyone
who has been in town that long. I made an exception because of Baker's being in the trade. It is still not
known, by the way, how the potato happened to fall
from the high-rise. Some literary critics believe that
Baker's muse dropped it. Some people who have columnists in the family, and thus know how sticky it can
get around the house when the columnist can't think
of an idea for a column, believe that Baker's wife
threw it. In fact, I threw it. It was meant as a general
warning: Never lower your guard.

Foreign Relations

September 22, 1984

NOW THAT I've established myself as an authority on foreign relations, you'll want to know if there is any significant difference between French people and Americans. Yes, I'm afraid there is. The difference is this: French people carry around dogs. That's right. I was over there in the spring, and I saw it with my own eyes. But even so, you may ask, aren't all of us — all people everywhere, regardless of nationality or race or sexual proclivity — brothers under the skin? No, not really. Sorry, but no. You can be a brother under the skin with someone who walks down the street with a doggie tucked under his arm like a loaf of sourdough rye if you want to. As for me, no thanks.

I believe most Americans would share my view. Americans don't carry dogs. I'd be the first to admit that they have their faults, but they don't carry dogs. Sure, an American may pick up a dog that has hurt its foot and carry it off to the vet. That's not the sort of dog-carrying I'm talking about. I'm talking about an otherwise respectable-looking Frenchman strolling down the street with a poodle in the crook of his arm, holding the poodle while having a drink at an outdoor cafe, shifting the poodle to the other arm when the check comes in order to get to his wallet and then continuing down the street carrying the poodle. That is what I would call carrying around a dog. A poodle is about as big a dog as I saw carried that way, but for all I know French people also lug around Dalmatians or Irish wolfhounds. It may be that if they intend to carry around an extremely large dog they get a friend to hold up one end. I don't know. Even an authority can't be expected to know everything. Whatever the size of the dog, you can imagine what happens if a canine-carrying Frenchman runs across an American tourist on the street: one of those confrontations that make foreign relations so messy. The American is likely to say, "Hey, guy, there somethin' the matter with your dog, or what?"

I worry a lot about these differences. I live in Canada in the summer — that is how I became an authority on foreign relations — and I worry a lot about the fact that Canadians use two-dollar bills. The United States quit using two-dollar bills a long time ago because everyone thought they were bad luck. How can we foster international understanding between Canadians and Americans when Canadians think nothing of paying for a pack of cigarettes with a bill that any American knows would cause him to lose the New York

State Lottery in perpetuity? A lot of Canadians must think that Americans are silly for being afraid of a two-dollar bill. Even worse, a lot of Canadians must worry about the possibility that the two-dollar bill is, in fact, unlucky. If not, they must wonder, Why is it that Canadians, who are widely considered to be much nicer than Americans, have a two-dollar bill that is worth only US $1.54?

What was that? Do French Canadians carry around dogs? I'm surprised by the question. Surprised and a little disappointed. It's just the sort of question that makes foreign relations so difficult. Of course French Canadians don't carry dogs. They don't even know that French people carry dogs. If they did, they might have all sorts of anxieties about whether they are wise to go on all the time about the importance of speaking French. So don't tell them.

In France, I would come home from the market — we had rented a house near a town called Saint-Rémy — and say to my wife, "I saw a man today with a briefcase in one hand and a fox terrier in the other. What hope can there be for the Atlantic alliance?"

"But how about the English?" my wife said, after one of those outbursts. "Aren't the English a lot like we are?"

"The English!" I said. "The English don't have mosquitoes! How can they understand the hopes and fears — mainly the fears — of Americans if they've never tried to fall asleep on a summer night when the buzzing starts?"

"But they went through the war," my wife said. "The blitz and all. And those Graham Greene Englishmen in tropical colonies who had malaria. Surely they must have —"

"The war is over," I said. "The empire is gone. All that's over now." Authorities learn never to get mired in the past. What I saw for the future was not pleasant: the NATO delegates are trying to meet, but the room is poisoned by suspicion and misunderstanding. The Canadian is wondering whether the British ambassador would sound quite so self-satisfied if he ever came face to face with the sort of Manitoba mosquito that is big enough to carry off a half-grown calf. The French ambassador is worried about the possibility that Canadian bad luck is transatlantically contagious. He starts to speak, but he's interrupted by the American who is commanding general of all NATO troops. "Your pooch break a leg?" the general asks. "Or what?"

Trying to soothe me with talk of small domestic details, my wife reminded me that I had to prepare the trash to take out early the next morning; she had learned that Tuesday is trash day in Saint-Rémy. "Odd," I said, "that's the same day I take out the trash in Canada. Also in New York." Then it hit me: International Trash Collection Day. Maybe we could all be brothers under the skin after all, thinking of each other as we hauled those big green plastic bags out to the curb. I was buoyed by that thought during the summer in Canada — until we were visited by a friend named Chester, who informed us that in New Haven, Connecticut, the trash is collected on Wednesday. I abandoned the notion of International Trash Collection Day without hesitation. An authority has to be ruthless about discarding unworkable theories.

Still, now and then I think back on those Canadian Tuesdays when I still thought that I.T.C.D. was what we authorities call a viable option. As I'd load my green plastic bags into a wheelbarrow, I would know that somewhere in England a cheerful Englishman — cheerful because he has just had a good night's sleep even without screens — was rolling his dustbin to the curb. Some New Yorker was cursing the sanitation men for having left a mess in front of his stoop. In France, a man was walking to the curb — a large green plastic bag in one arm, a nice little dog in the other.

name listed off to the side, so I got rid of the chart. I assume the President has taken down the one in the White House by now for the same reason.

It's also true that several years ago I publicly revealed what seemed to be a remarkable overlap in the operations of our family and those of the Carter White House: casting around for a way to define their Administration, the Carter people came up with a motto, A New Foundation, that we had already rejected during a search that eventually resulted in our family's adopting the motto Zip Up Your Jacket. That, I suspect, is the moment commentators have in mind when they say that at some point in the Carter Administration it became clear that Jimmy Carter was not exercising firm leadership of the American people. I might just add, by the way, that Carter would almost certainly have emerged in better shape from what is widely considered his most serious mistake in the 1980 presidential campaign debates — relating a discussion that he and his daughter, Amy, had about nuclear arms control — if he had ended the story by saying, "So I told my little daughter, Amy, 'Zip up your jacket.'"

Ronald Reagan seemed to be encouraging families to identify with the problems of the White House when, asked why American diplomats had moved into the embassy annex in Beirut before the installation of security devices had been completed, he said that anybody who has ever had a kitchen renovated knows that construction work is never finished when it's supposed to be. At first, I didn't see how that applied to our name listed off to the side, so I got rid of the chart. I assume the President has taken down the one in the White House by now for the same reason.

It's also true that several years ago I publicly revealed what seemed to be a remarkable overlap in the operations of our family and those of the Carter White House: casting around for a way to define their Administration, the Carter people came up with a motto, A New Foundation, that we had already rejected during a search that eventually resulted in our family's adopting the motto Zip Up Your Jacket. That, I suspect, is the moment commentators have in mind when they say that at some point in the Carter Administration it became clear that Jimmy Carter was not exercising firm leadership of the American people. I might just add, by the way, that Carter would almost certainly have emerged in better shape from what is widely considered his most serious mistake in the 1980 presidential campaign debates — relating a discussion that he and his daughter, Amy, had about nuclear arms control — if he had ended the story by saying, "So I told my little daughter, Amy, 'Zip up your jacket.' "

Ronald Reagan seemed to be encouraging families to identify with the problems of the White House when, asked why American diplomats had moved into the embassy annex in Beirut before the installation of security devices had been completed, he said that anybody who has ever had a kitchen renovated knows that construction work is never finished when it's supposed to be. At first, I didn't see how that applied to our family, since our kitchen is no longer being renovated. We managed to end the renovation in the late 1960s by employing a device we got from the Senate rather than the White House. Adapting the wise and lamentably ignored plan that Senator George Aiken had just put forward for ending the war in Vietnam, we declared ourselves victorious, even though a neutral observer might have concluded otherwise, and the contractor withdrew his troops. By chance, though, when the President made his comments about the Beirut embassy, the Palmers down the street were lacking only the delivery of their new restaurant-model six-burner stove and the sanding of their new butcher-block counters; sure enough, they returned from a weekend camping trip one Sunday night to find that a Moslem fanatic had suicide-bombed their kitchen. That's when I decided I'd better look into the possibility of our family having a line of the day.

I had learned about the line of the day from an article by Mark Hertsgaard in the *Village Voice*. Michael Deaver, the White House deputy chief of staff, told Hertsgaard that at an 8:15 meeting every morning, a line of the day is devised "to make sure we're all saying the same thing." After the meeting, another participant said, spokesmen throughout the government are told, "Here's what we're going to say; everybody say it at once. I don't care if you're asked the question or not." For instance, the line of the day might be "Far from being insulated by his aides, the President is out on the campaign trail fielding any questions the people want to ask." If so, spokesmen talk about the President's willingness to be grilled even if they are asked completely unrelated questions: whether the President still seems to be under the impression that Polaris is a denture cleanser, say, or whether it's true that the man most often mentioned around the White House for the next Supreme Court vacancy is best known in his hometown for his firm belief that he is in direct daily communication with the spirit of Frederick Barbarossa. (The President has, in fact, taken a number of questions lately, although usually from student audiences — first Republican college students, then high school students, then grade school students. So far, he hasn't taken on a play group, but if the scheduling continues in the direction it's going, one question the President may find himself fielding before the campaign's over is "Can I go make tinkle?")

I wish I knew how Deaver gets everybody to agree to say the same thing. We had a terrible time at our house. The closest thing to a precedent for a family line of the day I could think of was the custom of a friend of ours named Quinn, who, during a period of cash-flow problems, always answered the telephone by saying, "The check's in the mail" —which, by chance, is pretty close to what the White House's line of the day has been on what's being done about the deficit. My daughters wanted us to answer all questions by saying, "The snow is already fourteen inches deep, with drifts up to three feet." If enough people heard that enough times, they figured, school might be called off even though the temperature outside was seventy-two degrees.

Then the telephone rang. My wife answered. "It's the woman from Diners Club," she whispered, handing me the phone. "Tell her that the check's in the mail."

"Tell her the snow's already fourteen inches deep," my younger daughter said.

"Do you realize how quickly your credit rating can deteriorate?" the woman from Diners Club asked.

"Zip up your jacket," I replied.

Bananas, Presliced

October 13, 1984

WHILE I WAS in Brazil, I found out about presliced bananas. The discovery had no connection with the prevalence of bananas in Latin America, although Latin America would provide some good location shots if we decide to make a movie of all this. It wasn't that I found myself in an awkward social situation and tried to break the ice by saying, "Hey, is this one of those banana republics I've heard so much about?" The subject of presliced bananas actually came up quite unexpectedly at the tag end of a gathering in São Paulo. We were discussing hard-boiled eggs at the time.

I had just explained to one of the other guests that I can blow a hard-boiled egg out of the shell about seven times out of ten. (I learned that trick at Camp Osceola.) He responded by telling me that he could slice a banana without peeling it. You might say that we were in a bragging contest. I suppose I could have countered by saying that I can blow a hard-boiled egg out of the shell while standing on one leg — you'd be surprised how many people think that's more difficult than doing it with both feet on the ground — but he would probably just have tried to raise the stakes a bit by saying that he could peel an apple in one unbroken peel, a trick I consider to be of purely manual dexterity. Instead, I asked him how to preslice a banana. Escalation has to stop somewhere.

I realize that there are people who don't understand why I would be interested in presliced bananas — people who have never grasped the notion of pure science. "So what?" those people say when they read about some biologist who has discovered that boll weevils sweat. "What use is it?" If you grasp the notion of pure science, you can thirst for knowledge of presliced bananas for its own sake — although, as it happens, I was planning to use the knowledge to impress my daughters, who had shown indications of becoming blasé about the hard-boiled-egg trick ("Not again, Daddy"). I don't see the egg-blowing trick as part of the movie, by the way, except maybe as a sort of teaser before the credits.

Don't think that the diminished impact of the hard-boiled-egg trick left us with no science around the house. We happen to be one of those families that have stimulating scientific discussions at dinner most nights. We have talked about whether saccharin draws ants. We have talked about what sort of tweezers might be used to remove the caffeine from coffee beans. I noticed, though, that the last time I raised the caffeine-removal question my older daughter just smiled. She didn't say, "Talking about tweezers reflects a misunderstanding of the entire concept" or anything like that; she just smiled. I needed a new trick.

I had already decided against some common trick of purely manual dexterity, like peeling an apple in one unbroken peel — a decision I reached after spending some time behind closed doors with a sack of apples and a paring knife. That's why I came right out and asked the man in São Paulo how to preslice a banana. He told me that you use a needle and thread. That surprised me. Just for a moment there, I let myself think that maybe caffeine is removed from coffee beans with a needle and thread, but I couldn't really see it. To preslice a banana, the man told me, you circumscribe the banana in several stitches just under the skin, being careful to put the needle back into the hole it just came out of; at the final stitch, you bring the needle out of the first hole, and then pull both ends of the thread, severing the banana inside the peel. The banana remains unmarked. When people speak of the wonders of nature, the man in São Paulo told me, they should include the miraculous speed at which a banana skin seals over a needle hole.

I needed practice. By chance, I had to spend a week in Texas just after I returned from Brazil. If this is going to be one of those technicolor movies that goes from exotic setting to exotic setting, Texas would be good. First, you have an establishing shot of the vast Texas horizon, with the camera pulling back slowly to show a Holiday Inn. Then there's an interior shot: A man is sitting inside his motel room, going at a banana with a needle and thread. Occasionally, he grimaces; the needle has rubbed up against an old paring-knife wound. Then there is one of those shots of an airplane taking off. We see a plane full of businessmen — clicking their calculators, snapping and unsnapping their attaché cases. One of the businessmen turns to the traveler next to him. "I couldn't help noticing that you're sewing a banana," the businessman says.

"It passes the time," the traveler replies.

When I arrived home from Texas late one night, I handed my wife a banana. "It's presliced," I said.

"Oh, did the girls tell you about that?" my wife said.

"The girls?"

"They do it with a needle and thread," she said. "I think they learned it from that book *Fun 'n' Play for a Rainy Day.*"

"I learned it in São Paulo," I said. "São Paulo, Brazil."

"Well, it must be all around then," she said. She peeled the banana and started to eat it.

But that's no way to end a technicolor movie — with a grown woman eating a presliced banana. In the movie, the traveler would present his family with "some of these new presliced bananas from Brazil," provoking a stimulating scientific discussion about how Brazilian agronomists grow bananas presliced.

Maybe workers tie strings around newly sprouted bananas, and as the bananas grow the strings cut through them, the traveler suggests. The strings are not noticeable because they are themselves made out of bananas — those stringy things you sometimes pull off a banana before eating it. Other theories are offered. Then the traveler reveals that he is the one who presliced the banana. It's a trick. His daughters are impressed. They say that some people's fathers can only do tricks like peeling an apple in one unbroken peel. "Show us, Daddy!" they say. The traveler preslices a banana for his daughters. Then he does it standing on one leg. Fade out.